AFTER THE DELUGE

AFTER THE DELUGE

Essays Towards the Desecularization
of the Church

edited by William Oddie

First published in Great Britain 1987
SPCK
Holy Trinity Church
Marylebone Road
London NW1 4DU

British Library Cataloguing in Publication Data

After the deluge : essays towards the
  desecularization of the church.
  1. Theology
  I. Oddie, William
  230   BR118

  ISBN 0-281-04258-6

Photoset and printed in Great Britain by
WBC Print Ltd, Bristol

CONTENTS

CONTRIBUTORS

WILLIAM ODDIE is an Anglican parish priest. Until 1985 he was a Librarian of Pusey House and Fellow of St Cross College, Oxford. Dr Oddie is a literary historian and theologian, and is a regular commentator on television, radio, and in the press. He is the author of *What Will Happen to God?* (SPCK 1984), a controversial examination of feminist theology.

ROGER BECKWITH is Warden of Latimer House and Lecturer in Liturgy at Wycliffe Hall, Oxford. He is a frequent contributor to scholarly journals and other publications, and is widely regarded as a leading spokesman for the Evangelical wing of the Church of England. His major work of scholarship, *The Old Testament Canon of the New Testament Church*, was published in 1986 by SPCK.

WAYNE HANKEY is Associate Professor of Classics at Dalhousie University and at King's College, Halifax, Canada. He is also Librarian of King's College. Dr Hankey read Theology at Trinity College, Toronto, and at St Peter's College, Oxford. His study of the *Summa Theologiae* of St Thomas Aquinas entitled *God in Himself* was published in 1986 by Oxford University Press.

PETER HODGSON is Senior Research Fellow at Corpus Christi College and Lecturer in Nuclear Physics at the University of Oxford. He has published many books and papers on nuclear physics, the most recent being *Our Nuclear Future?* (Marshall Pickering 1984).

GRAHAM LEONARD is the Bishop of London. He was consecrated Bishop of Willesden in 1964, and was Bishop of Truro from 1973 to 1981. He is Chairman of the General Synod Board of Education, and is the author of several books, including *Firmly I Believe and Truly*

(Mowbray 1985). A Catholic with an Evangelical upbringing, he believes that true radicalism springs from the application of orthodox doctrine.

JAMES MUNSON is a full-time writer. He read History at Oxford where, in 1969, he was awarded the Thomas Arnold Historical Prize. In 1975 he received his Oxford doctorate. After teaching history for several years in the University he devoted all his time to writing, and is well known for his contributions to a wide range of journals and newspapers. He has also written or presented some twenty-five programmes for the BBC.

ACKNOWLEDGEMENTS

Extracts from *The Dilemma of Democracy* by Lord Hailsham are reprinted by permission of Collins Publishers.

Extracts from *Politics and the Pursuit of Happiness* by Ghita Ionescu are reprinted by permission of the Longman Group Ltd.

Extracts from *Something Beautiful for God* by Malcolm Muggeridge are reprinted by permission of Collins Publishers.

Extracts from *The Other Side of 1984* by Lesslie Newbigin are reprinted by permission of WCC Publications.

Introduction

WILLIAM ODDIE

As the twentieth century draws to a close, it becomes increasingly clear that the Christian Church in the Western world faces a deeper internal crisis than at any time since that which led up to the Protestant Reformation. Now, as then, many if not most of those charged with the leadership of Western Christendom are remote from the beliefs and assumptions of those who look to them for spiritual sustenance. Now too, and to an even greater extent than in the sixteenth and seventeenth centuries, there is a profound division within the Church over the actual nature and content of the Christian faith itself.

THE HIDDEN CRISIS

The crisis, of course, does not *seem* as serious as that which led to the great human and political convulsions of the Reformation and Counter-Reformation. In the great controversy of our own times, those ranged on both sides command no armies; and the secularization of European societies has made such questions appear (to the non-combatant) to be no more than a matter of the tensions which are inevitable between alternative – and equally unverifiable – subjective views.

The crisis, furthermore, has not yet manifested itself in any major visible schism. None the less, if schism is that division which occurs within communities of faith between people who have irreconcilable convictions over quite fundamental religious questions, then schism there is, transcending Christendom's historic divisions, all the more debilitating for its implicit and trans-institutional character.

Nor can the defence of 'pluralism' or 'comprehensiveness' be put forward to justify the present situation: in the words of a 1968 Lambeth Conference report, 'comprehensiveness demands agreement on fundamentals, while tolerating disagreement on matters

1

in which Christians may differ . . .'[1] It has to be said that most Christian communions in the West display no such agreement on fundamentals, and it might be added that in English-speaking countries it tends to be Anglicanism which most vividly demonstrates how such a lack of agreement can affect the Church's credibility, particularly for non-believers. The Roman Catholic Church is in general the one exception to this tendency, though even here, as we shall see, we need to enter some reservations.

Two signs of crisis may be singled out. First, the growing division between the faithful in the parishes and many of those who speak for the Church at a national or institutional level. These spokesmen include the bishops, whose historic function is that of chief pastor and defender of the tradition, a function which (despite many honourable exceptions) appears decreasingly exercised as a first priority.

They include, too, new hierarchies of influence: on the one hand, the various church assemblies and bureaucracies which have multiplied over the last three decades; and on the other, a rather different (though overlapping) kind of inner circle, whose membership is made up of those who are still generally taken in the West as representing the authentic voice of theological inquiry.

The second sign of crisis is that the mainline Western Churches not only fail in any significant numbers to attract new converts, but actually continue to lose committed support at a time when a real cultural shift is occurring, in a civilization less and less prepared to accept the rationalist norms of the last century and a half. We live at a time when it is increasingly apparent that there is, to employ Professor Keith Ward's description, a 'turn of the tide'.[2] In 1851, Matthew Arnold had mournfully registered the effects of an earlier turn (the tide flowing the other way), in his famous lines from *Dover Beach*:

> The Sea of Faith
> Was once . . . at the full, and round earth's shore
> Lay like the folds of a bright girdle furled.
> But now I only hear
> Its melancholy, long, withdrawing roar,
> Retreating . . .

The Victorian Rationalism partly responsible for effecting this retreat was not something whose effects Arnold anticipated with any pleasure; the controlled and ever-brightening future foretold by the Victorians

2

in their more optimistic moments was, as he only too correctly surmised, a vaporous fantasy;

> . . . the world, which seems
> To lie before us like a land of dreams,
> So various, so beautiful, so new,
> Hath really neither joy, nor love, nor light,
> Nor certitude, nor peace, nor help for pain . . .

Today, such dreams, together with the Victorian Rationalism that spawned them, have collapsed within Western civilization. They remain intact, however, in certain milieux – most importantly for us, among liberal modernist theologians and in the various establishments and bureaucracies whose ideological underpinning they still supply. In such circles, the 'turn of the tide' remains steadfastly unobserved; the antique philosophical assumptions they continue to employ, indeed, have often in recent years formed the basis for efforts at 'renewing' the Church, sometimes paradoxically accompanying attempts (particularly within the Roman Catholic Church) at recovering a genuinely biblical faith. It becomes increasingly difficult to avoid the strong impression that those who speak most frequently about the need for 'relevance' and for the Church to be receptive to modern knowledge are in fact often those most out of touch with contemporary reality and unacquainted with recent (as opposed to late-Victorian and early-twentieth-century) thinking.

THE SEARCH FOR RELEVANCE

The search for relevance to secular culture has led to bizarre results, particularly in attempts to 'humanize' the liturgy. This writer recalls, during a visit to America in 1985, reading a news report (undoubtedly accurate) about a Roman Catholic priest who had had to be restrained by his bishop from conducting a mass baptism for 'cabbage patch' dolls. Such excesses, of course, have always been the exception rather than the rule, and in the Roman Catholic Church at least were far more common during the 1970s (the decade of Peter Hebblethwaite's book *The Runaway Church* (1975)) than the 1980s.

The simple fact is, however, that incidents of this kind, perpetrated by jaunty clerics of all persuasions, have (not entirely without reason) been understood by outsiders as being more indiscreet than unrepresentative. They demonstrate, it has often seemed, the underlying fact that the Churches – having lost confidence in divine revelation as their principal source of inspiration – have now decided to communicate with a secular age on its own terms: if you can't beat them, join them. Malcolm Muggeridge, a distinguished and in some ways representative example of the late-twentieth-century movement from secular humanist scepticism to religious hunger, gave in the early 1970s the following reason for his refusal to become (at that time) a member of the Roman Church – reservations which he made plain applied with even greater force to other parts of the Christian Church also:

> . . . if I were a member, then I should be forced to say that, in my opinion, if men were to be stationed at the doors of the Churches with whips to drive worshippers away, or inside the religious orders specifically to discourage vocations, or among the clergy to spread alarm and despondency, they could not hope to be as effective in achieving these ends as are trends and policies seemingly now dominant within the Church. Feeling so, it would be preposterous to seek admission, more particularly as, if the ecumenical course is fully run, luminaries of the [Anglican] Church to which I nominally belong, like the former Bishop of Woolwich [John Robinson] . . . will in due course take their place in the Roman Catholic hierarchy among the heirs of St Peter.[3]

When every allowance has been made for over-reaction and journalistic excess; when the positive and necessary aspects of *aggiornamento* and its non-Roman Catholic equivalents have been fully recognized; when everything has been said to establish that it is well understood by all concerned that the Christian Church must speak to its own times; when all this has been said and done, the fact remains that for those who are outside the Church but nevertheless religiously aware, what Muggeridge calls 'trends and policies now seemingly dominant within the Church' have made Christianity – if anything – less, and not more, likely to attract them. Most of those former sceptics who have come to the conclusion that there may be such a thing as ultimate or transcendent meaning in human existence are not looking for it in the Christian Church.

The reason for this is not far to seek. The Christian Church in the West, at the level of the various hierarchies of influence we have discussed, quite simply finds the idea of transcendent or ultimate meaning (let alone actual divine intervention in human affairs) an embarrassment to its search for relevance to what it takes to be an age wholly secular in its instincts and assumptions.

Any idea to the contrary tends to be firmly put in its place. Hence, during a discussion in the Church of England's General Synod, one speaker suggested that the report *Faith in the City* relied too exclusively on a secular, socio-political perspective, and suggested an amendment affirming that 'individual lives and attitudes were transformed' through 'the reconciling love of Christ'. This surely unexceptionable proposal was hotly contested, and the amendment was lost:

> Canon Colin Craston (Manchester) opposed Mr Godin's amend-
> ment, saying that there was an agenda to be pursued – the
> establishment of justice and the building of community – *before*
> the good news of the life-changing grace of Christ *could be*
> proclaimed.[4] (My emphasis)

The grace of God is thus seen as dependent on prior human action, and on the pre-existence of a just human society: it would be difficult to imagine any assumption more directly opposed to the faith of the New Testament Church, or to the experience of the numberless multitude of those reborn in Christ who down the Christian years have survived – and have even been strengthened by – persecution, injustice and degradation, through the power of his Spirit. There was a risk, said the senior churchman whose duty it was to administer the *coup de grâce* to Mr Godin's amendment, that it would be seen as 'desperately pietistic'.[5]

To a secularized Christianity of this kind, the work – say – of a Mother Teresa of Calcutta is marginal, even meaningless, offering in itself no structural change in society, only the reality and the example of a luminous Christian love for the poor; admirable in its way, no doubt, but 'desperately pietistic'. And yet, ironically, in an age when the Church is so obsessed by its inability to carry conviction in a secular culture, it is probably this frail old peasant woman who has focused the world's attention on the world's poor, not as a political class but as the children of God, more powerfully than all the 'liberation' theologians put together.

William Oddie

NOT IN THE WISDOM OF MEN

More, however, needs to be said: that it is her kind of faith alone, one centred on a reality beyond this world and this life, which (as Malcolm Muggeridge found) carries conviction with sceptics and unbelievers in a secular age. After Muggeridge had interviewed Mother Teresa for the first time on television, the public response was overwhelming: here, as Muggeridge commented afterwards, was the answer to the problem of conveying Christianity through the mass media:

> Just get on the screen a face shining and overflowing with Christian love; someone for whom the world is nothing and the service of Christ everything; someone reborn out of servitude to the ego and the flesh, and into the glorious liberty of the children of God. Then it doesn't matter how the face is lighted or shot; whether in front or profile, close-up or two-shot or long-shot; what questions are put, or by whom . . . it might seem surprising, on the face of it, that an obscure nun of Albanian origins, very nervous . . . should reach English viewers on a Sunday evening as no professional Christian apologist, bishop or archbishop, moderator or knockabout progressive dog-collared demonstrator ever has . . . The message was the same message that was heard in the world for the first time two thousand years ago; as Mother Teresa showed, it has not changed its sense or lost its magic. As then, so now, it is bought, 'not with enticing words of man's wisdom, but in demonstration of the Spirit and of power; that your faith should not stand in the wisdom of men, but in the power of God'.[6]

It is not enough to say, as is undoubtedly true, that the characterization so far offered here of the condition of the contemporary Church is to some extent oversimplified. It is certainly necessary to assert that 'faith . . . not . . . in the wisdom of men but in the power of God' is powerfully alive in the Church today wherever men and women open themselves to it. This can frequently be seen in local Christian communities – many of which are growing rapidly while the Church as a whole steadily continues to contract. It is also true that in their personal spirituality, many of those who form part of what I have described as 'hierarchies of influence' are devout, even traditional. Nevertheless, it has to be said that in its institutional character,

6

the Church appears to the world (and appearances are all too often a true guide) to base its *thinking* – in both doctrinal and social questions – firmly on the 'wisdom of men' alone.

It is this, far more than any feeling that the Church should 'keep out of politics', which robs its pronouncements on social affairs of their credibility. As a leading article in one major English daily put it, having rightly stated that 'Christianity is in its essence a belief . . . having a necessary social dimension':

> The question is whether the understanding of society demonstrated by – say – a document such as *Faith in the City* owes anything *at a fundamental level* to a supernatural understanding of human life, and whether or not precisely the same conclusions might not have emerged from a meeting of the British Humanist Association. The main problem is not whether the document is Marxist in its assumptions . . . The problem is whether or not such documents owe anything whatsoever to a specifically Christian understanding. Producing biblical quotations in support of secular arguments proves nothing.[7]

That the Church was in 'deep crisis', thought the writer, was 'increasingly clear'. 'At a time', he continued, 'when industrialized man, weary of being the plaything of large-scale social processes . . . is prepared to turn back to religion more than at any time during the last half-century, the Church is becoming more and more committed to a collectivized understanding of society, and a non-supernatural version of traditional Christian doctrine.'[8]

The Church has always known (and when it has forgotten, disaster has always sooner or later been the inevitable result) that to invest too heavily in the guiding tenets of any culture always brings the risk of sudden bankruptcy when these beliefs begin to collapse. 'The Church which is married to the Spirit of the Age', wrote Dean Inge, 'will be a widow in the next.' This is always true, even at times of apparent stability, for the Spirit of the Age is always ephemeral, however solid and definitive its assumptions may appear at the time. At such periods, though, change may come slowly enough for adjustments to be made, so that the Church's involvement in now-discarded ideas may be forgotten. But at times of rapid change, the risk of isolation and collapse is particularly high. A society which begins to make the bitter discovery that the beliefs on which it has built its whole understanding of human existence have led it into the valley of the shadow of death, will not look for guidance to those who have themselves proved blind.

THE END OF RENAISSANCE MAN

There is every reason for supposing that now, as we begin to approach the end of the second millennium since the birth of Christ, such a period of disillusion and uncertainty is already upon us. We may well be arriving, that is to say, not merely at a *fin de siècle*, but at a watershed in human history altogether more momentous than any such phrase can convey. One observer has said, quite simply, that 'we have come to the end of Renaissance man'.[9]

Whatever reservations we may have over such judgements (as with similar oversimplifications to do with 'the Enlightenment'), it is increasingly clear that they have to be taken seriously. Their underlying sense, perhaps, more and more a simple matter of general observation, is that we have come to a time when there is, inescapably, little rational cause for supposing that humanity has 'come of age'. Indeed, if we think of the circumstances in which Bonhoeffer, imprisoned in Hitler's Germany, originally used the phrase, we must surely be struck, above all, by its inappropriateness.

It is, in the end, the remoteness from reality of the liberal secularist approach which is its most remarkable feature – ironically so, since it is precisely a responsiveness to the intellectual climate of the passing age which is its most vaunted claim. Somehow, despite the political and intellectual history of the twentieth century, the secularist faith in what one writer has called 'the religion of progress'[10] remains unclouded.

And yet, if one thing is certain, it is surely this: that whether in the East or in the West, the world's 'advanced' industrialized cultures, built on the belief that man could control his environment and his destiny, have come to the end of their belief in themselves. We can say, too, that this loss of faith has been gathering momentum for at least the last century, and probably for longer than that. In what was already being seen as one of the seminal works of the 1980s soon after its publication, Bishop Lesslie Newbigin followed Michael Polanyi in suggesting a parallel between classical culture in the time of St Augustine and that of our own time:

There are obvious parallels between our situation and that of St Augustine. We stand at what feels like the end of a period of extraordinary brilliance. The feeling of being 'at the end' is . . . I have suggested, the feeling that our culture has no future and that life has no meaning. The classical culture which was disintegrating in St Augustine's day was the one to which the Enlightenment sought to return. It was the vision of the Greek philosophers and the Roman law-givers, not that of the biblical prophets and apostles, which inspired the age of which we are the heirs. If we, too, have come to a point where our culture seems to have no future, if our young people are tempted to turn their backs on the whole magnificent European adventure and seek for meaning among the a-historical mysticisms of Asia, if the immense achievements of autonomous reason seem to have produced a world which is at best meaningless and at worst full of demons, then it could be that Polanyi is right, that we shall not find renewal within the framework of the assumptions which the men of the Enlightenment held to be 'self-evident', that there is needed a radical conversion, a new starting-point which begins as an act of trust in divine grace as something simply given to be received in faith and gratitude.[11]

The authors of this book have started from the conviction that such a new starting-point is urgently needed, and that the 'radical conversion' of which Bishop Newbigin writes is needed most urgently of all within the Church itself. This will not involve any obscurantist rejection of reason: for St Augustine, classical learning was a tool to be used, not an idol to be cast down. Nor will it lead to any withdrawal from the social dimension of Christian belief. But it *will* mean the restoration of the Augustinian perception that faith, a free gift of God to those who seek it in true poverty of spirit, is to be seen as the *beginning* of the Church's intellectual journey, and not its hoped-for end; and a first priority towards this restoration is that the liberal secularist reversal of this essential Christian assumption should itself be reversed.

Before we can do this, however, we need to understand how it is that the Church comes to be where it now stands. How is it that the Church can – to the extent that it does – rely on 'the wisdom of men' rather than on 'the power of God' as he has revealed it, not (as to a greater or lesser extent it always has done) as a matter of manifest human sinfulness to be acknowledged with penitence and corrected by reform, but as a settled intellectual habit openly defended? To put the question more succinctly, how did the Church come to be secularized to the extent that it is?

THE SWINGING SIXTIES

Perhaps the easiest way to begin an answer to the question is to return to the 1960s, to the decade when the intellectual habits and convictions of so many of the present generation of church leaders were formed or confirmed. For it was at this time more than at any other before or since that 'secularization' could be openly promoted as a process to be accepted by the Church as inevitable and therefore to be encouraged, rather than as an ever-present danger from which it should guard itself. 'It will do no good', wrote Harvey Cox in 1965, 'to cling to our religious and metaphysical versions of Christianity in the hope that one day religion and metaphysics will once again be back. They are disappearing for ever.'[12] To many, possibly most, of those actively involved during the 1960s in the debate over 'secular Christianity', Cox's analysis, quoted, of course, from his famous book *The Secular City*, was self-evident, and the process it described wholly beneficial.

The secularization of theology was seen as part of an inevitable process, 'a positive advance', as a popular survey by John Bowden and James Richmond put it, 'which has its roots in Christianity, and sets out to reinterpret Christian thought and reshape Christian practice, in the light of the present situation'. Those who swam against the tide as, with characteristic intellectual tenacity did Fr Eric Mascall in his book *The Secularisation of Christianity* (also published in 1965) they dismissed with ill-disguised impatience as 'negative'.[13]

Bonhoeffer's famous phrase, already quoted, became a watchword of the movement: 'Mankind' had 'come of age';[14] how then could anyone prepared to stand out against the trend be regarded as anything but spiritually immature and cut off from reality? 'Secularisation', pronounced Cox, 'rolls on, and if we are to understand and communicate with our present age, we must learn to love it in its unremitting secularity. We must learn, as Bonhoeffer said, to speak of God in a secular fashion and find a non-religious interpretation of religious concepts.'[15]

Twenty years later, there were few left who were prepared to speak in such stark and certain tones. Cox himself had written what reads at times remarkably like a recantation, in his suggestively entitled book *Religion in the Secular City: Towards a Post-modern Theology* (1984). The problem, Cox now believed, was that

> . . . the world of declining religion to which my earlier book was addressed has begun to change in ways that few people anticipated. A new age that some call the 'post-modern' has begun to appear. No one is quite sure just what the postmodern era will be like, but one thing seems quite clear. Rather than an age of rampant secularization and religious decline, it appears to be more of an era of religious revival and the return of the sacral. No one talks much today about the long night of religion . . .[16]

Certainly, the great classics of the secularizing tendency – *The Secular City* itself, John Robinson's *Honest to God* (1963), Ronald Gregor Smith's *Secular Christianity* (1966), Paul van Buren's *Secular Meaning of the Gospel* (1963) – have about them the appearance of monuments to an age now definitively past. They seem, indeed, almost as quaint and remote as the relics of the parallel 'Death of God' movement. Almost but not quite: for though it is now quite clear that reports of the death of God have been wholly premature, it is by no means equally apparent that the fundamental question addressed by the secular Christianity school of theology – 'what Christianity really is, or indeed who Christ really is, for us today' (Bonhoeffer)[17] – is, or ought to be, asked any less insistently today. It is, however, now evident that many of the diagnoses so confidently proffered in the 1960s were based on an entire misunderstanding of the historical nature of the case.

There may be another reason, nevertheless, why we cannot yet write off 'secular Christianity' as a now defunct theological fashion, safely to be located in a chapter entitled 'The 1960s' in some future history of Christian doctrine in the twentieth century. For if we understand Robinson and Cox and van Buren, and (more importantly) their origins, particularly in the late speculations of Bonhoeffer himself, not as offering a *prescriptive* theology, a theology for the necessary future of the Church if Christianity in the West is to regain its persuasiveness for the surrounding culture, but as having on the contrary a *descriptive* character, indicating in certain essentials the boundaries inside which already theological discourse over the last century and a half has tacitly

11

more and more established itself, we discover that these dusty volumes take on an entirely different aspect. We find that if we are to judge the Church's real beliefs not so much by what it is prepared more or less – often less – convincingly to argue, as by what has truly entered into the tacit assumptions of its spokesmen (official or self-appointed), then by the 1960s Cox's revolution was already in place within Western Christendom, despite the persistence of counter-revolutionary elements among the clerical caste who had established it.

THE NATURE OF THE PROBLEM

What is it that has happened? Is it necessarily a bad thing that it has? We can scarcely quarrel with attempts to answer Bonhoeffer's question as to 'what Christianity really is . . . for us today'. It has been, through the ages, the starting-point for all authentic theological endeavour, and the difficulties of facing it in the context of a secularized urban culture are not to be underestimated. The problem for Christianity now is to remain itself while communicating with a culture whose assumptions are no longer Christian ones; to be aware of the process of the continuing secularization of society in such a way that, as Fr Bernard Häring puts it, 'we will be in a strategic position to commit ourselves so as not to degenerate into "secularism" while grasping wholeheartedly the just exigencies of "secularity". Within a perspective of faith and vigilance for the "signs of the times", secularization will then be transformed into a propitious opportunity, a true *kairos* [time of favour] for the people of God'.[18]

It is clear enough, however, (though few would actually realize there was anything in Fr Häring's strategy they disagreed with) that it has in practice commonly operated in reverse, so that the Christian mind, far from transforming secularization, has itself been profoundly affected by it. For Cox and his school, this was a process fervently to be encouraged. The values and attitudes of the *saeculum*, of the present age, were to become determinative not only of the way in which apologetic strategy was to *convey* religious truth, but also of the actual content and substance of what was to be conveyed. 'Secularization', said Cox, 'is man turning his attention away from worlds beyond and towards this world and this time.'[19] This seemed to many an obviously good idea, and this broad understanding of what was involved in the secularizing process was, on the whole, shared by those unsympathetic to it. Eric Mascall's definition of 'the secular' was 'that whole body of thought and activity which is concerned with man's life in what is sometimes called "this world" . . . Thus there is excluded from the sphere of "the secular" any concern which a man may have with a possible future life after death and any concern which he may have, even during "this life", with an order of reality (if such there be) which transcends the experience of the senses'. He added that 'of course, a man may believe in the reality and importance of the secular without being a secularist'.[20]

What Cox and others failed adequately to perceive at the time was the extent to which the secularization of the Christian mind was already nearing the end of a long period of incubation, so that it was by now nearly (but not quite) endemic in contemporary theological speculation. Hence, David Jenkins, writing in 1966, could assail Tillich for his

> . . . failure to recognize (what Bonhoeffer came to stress) that the immediate possibilities and questions open to modern man are so many, so rich, and so satisfying that for many people ultimate questions just do not arise and that to hanker after them is held to be an immature refusal to accept that immediate questions put us on to that which is truly valuable and that this valuableness is none the less valuable for being, inevitably, limited and 'non-ultimate'.[21]

We can gain some idea of the extent of what has happened to Christian perceptions over the last 150 years, by comparing this passage with another, by John Henry Newman. It is from a sermon delivered during the 1830s by the Anglican Newman in his Tractarian phase; but it could equally well evoke his evangelical roots or his final Roman Catholic position. It is, in fact, in any historical perspective, normative Christian belief, held in one way or another by the Fathers, the medieval doctors, the Reformers and the Counter-Reformers alike:

> As the traveller on serious business may be tempted to linger, while he gazes on the beauty of the prospect which opens on his way, so this well-ordered and divinely governed world, with all its blessings of sense and knowledge, may lead us to neglect those interests which will endure when itself has passed away. In truth, it promises more than it can fulfil.

13

... And hence it is that many pursuits in themselves honest and right, are nevertheless to be engaged in with caution, lest they seduce us; and those perhaps with special caution, which tend to the well-being of men in this life. The sciences, for instance, of good government, acquiring wealth, of preventing and relieving want, and the like, are for this reason especially dangerous; for fixing, as they do, our exertions on this world as an end, they go far to persuade us that they have no other end ...[22]

In the words of the Epistle to the Hebrews, 'here have we no abiding city, but we seek one that is to come' (13.14).

It is important to note that Newman is not adopting what is sometimes described by modern Christian writers as a 'pietist' or 'world-denying' posture. He, and the Christian tradition he here represents, fully accept the 'reality and importance of the secular': 'the world', says Newman, '... is framed ... by God Himself, and therefore cannot be otherwise than good': this applies, too, to the world's 'blessings of sense and knowledge'.[23] The world, nevertheless, is not our ultimate destination; and if we suppose that it is, then, (we might add) even to the world we can have little to say that the world cannot discover for itself.

THE NEW CONVENTIONAL WISDOM

It is clear enough that in the century and a half that has unfolded since Newman's words were spoken, there has been an immense shift in the Western Christian tradition (if, indeed, 'tradition' is the right word to continue to use). What is it that has happened? Are we right to describe the process as a gradual secularization of Christianity, a process in which theology has in a variety of different ways succumbed to secular trends which it ought to have resisted? What, for that matter, *is* secularization? Above all, we need to guard against assuming too readily that something at all simple to describe has taken place. Even more, perhaps, must we be wary of the ever-present danger of supposing that whatever did happen was inevitable, or that the history of our times, including its intellectual history, could not have developed in a very different way. Certainly, it is not wholly *untrue* to say that the last 150 years have been a period of steady and irreversible enlightenment and progress (a notion which has contributed greatly to the force and prestige of 'secular' ideas among theologians). But neither is this proposition wholly *true*. Without doubt, we can often, over the last two centuries, observe error driven out by truth; but as we do, we not infrequently espy error replacing error, and, as often, old truth discarded for freshly minted illusion.

It is a confused picture. Old superstitions die; but sometimes new ones take their place: very different superstitions, perhaps, but superstitions none the less, if superstition be the holding of irrational beliefs which have all the prescriptive strength of entrenched habit. The very quest for freedom from error and illusion breeds its own fantasies. The secularization of Western culture is not simply an observable trend: it is also a movement; and movements are always prone to the spawning of legends and heroic confrontations. The first Secular Society was founded in 1851: but secularism as a moral attitude has its roots in the anti-clericalism of the Enlightenment, with its touching faith that the simple application of science, 'nature', and 'reason' to the affairs of men would sweep away the dead hand of tradition and lead irresistibly to a more rational and humane society. Science and religion, above all, are seen in this mythology as natural enemies, symbolic antagonists in the great historical drama whose happy dénouement is to be the advent of 'humanity come of age'.

C. A. Watts, the founder of the Rationalist Press Association, epitomizes the high moral tone of Victorian secularism, and also the way in which reason and faith could now be seen as natural antagonists: for Watts, it is natural to antithesize the scientist, seen as a moral force, by the figure of Christ himself, not to the latter's advantage: 'He revealed nothing of practical value, and taught no virtues that were before unknown. . . He taught false notions of existence; he had no knowledge of science. . . He lacked experimental force. . .'[24]

The new orthodoxy was propagated by popular works like John William Draper's *History of the Conflict between Religion and Science* (1874) – obscure now, but not without its successes: translated into eight languages, placed on the *index librorum prohibitorum* and a century later perused by Professor Owen Chadwick. The conflict, observes Professor Chadwick, 'was hypostasized, science and religion were blown up into balloon duellists, science containing all knowledge, religion containing no knowledge, and the two set side by side, with

15

know-nothing using sabre to keep know-all from his place. Once it had been hypostasized, it became possible to read back the antipathy throughout history, and see the ding-dong of duel through centuries, science invented by the Macedonian campaigns of Alexander the Great, Christianity suppressing the schools of Alexandria which were schools of science, Church putting earth at the centre of the universe and Galileo proving it was not, Church still talking of "incessant divine intervention" and science talking of the "operation of primordial and unchangeable law".'[25]

Science, unlike theology, seemed precise and verifiable; real knowledge (though sometimes forbidding and impersonal) rather than fantasy, however comforting. Now that it had freed itself from the control of ecclesiastical ideology (not the same thing as theology), the relationship of science with religion seemed not so much dissolved as inverted. Science had been secularized; and now it was in a position to secularize in its turn. Scientists, it seemed, might now claim (certainly, many claimed for them), in the words of a modern politician fresh to power, that 'we are the masters now'. Henceforth, in a great and growing polarization, theology would more and more submit itself to the tutelage of 'science' (of science, that is, understood in a certain way) or it would declare science to be irrelevant or even inimical to supernatural faith, and therefore to be either ignored or anathematized. There were, and are, other alternatives: but they hardly affected the popular understanding, and hardly more the theological debate.

NEW SUPERSTITIONS FOR OLD

Nowhere can we see the replacement of old superstitions with new more clearly than in the context of this entire question of how science and religion can be seen to affect one another. That the one influences the other is hardly a nineteenth-century discovery: Galileo was condemned not for bad astronomy, but for heresy. The original error was a theological one: to suppose that, since man had been made in the image of God, and since also God had become man, had died and risen again here on this earth, and since it followed from this that the earth was at the centre of God's purposes for his creation, that *therefore* the very motion of the planets in their courses must enact this theological truth. As though in some morality play, the creation must crudely mimic the truths of revelation: it is the very stuff of which superstition and bigotry are made. And yet, curiously, it was not this bizarre conception that was swept away by the advent of Copernican astronomy. The idea of cosmic mimicry survived into the Victorian age and beyond to fuse with the popular mythology surrounding the theory of evolution; but now, since it was proved that the earth revolved around the sun, it must be either that man himself, far from being at the centre of God's purposes, was simply part of nature, evolved and not created, or at the least that God (if he existed) was not a being to whom man could look any longer for help: the supernatural order and the natural order did not interlock; man and nature could and must survive alone. The irrationality is just as rank: indeed, it is precisely the same irrationality, now inverted. 'God made Man, therefore Man is central, therefore the sun revolves around the earth', becomes 'the earth revolves around the sun, therefore man is peripheral, therefore God is not actively involved in man's affairs'. It is the same superstition, still alive and believed; here is one of its modern exponents, the Revd Don Cupitt:

> . . . although we have a natural and childish tendency to see everything as revolving around ourselves and as existing for our sakes, the truth is rather that we are marginal in the cosmos. During the Victorian period the steady extension of the cosmic time-scale and the triumph of Darwinism rammed home the Copernican lesson: man is wholly a product of nature and has no objective reason for claiming any special significance in nature.[26]

Darwinism, of course, from the beginning, by no means struck everyone as claiming either that man was simply part of nature, the result (in Bertrand Russell's striking phrase) of 'accidental collocations of atoms',[27] or that nature itself was independent of supernatural causation, or even that science and traditional religion were opposed. Undoubtedly, many not insubstantial personages on both sides of the argument thought so: Bishop Wilberforce (most famously) among 'conservative' churchmen; among the scientists, Darwinians like John Tyndall and G. J. Romanes. Other scientists, like Huxley, were far from claiming that Darwin in particular or scientific discovery in general had disproved religion. Churchmen were equally divided as to the implications of the theory of evolution. H. P. Liddon, no theological liberal, thought it 'merely one way of describing what we can observe of God's continuous action upon the physical world';[28]

Dean Church thought it 'wonderful "shortness of thought" to treat the theory itself as incompatible with ideas of a higher and spiritual order'.[29] Nevertheless, the effect, often poignant, of what were seen by many as the irresistible implications of scientific discovery on religious faith may be observed more and more frequently as the century wears on. Romanes, a former evangelical 'converted' after a correspondence with Darwin himself, wrote in 1878 of 'the appalling contrast between the hallowed glory of that creed which once was mine, and the lonely mystery of existence as now I find it. . .'.[30]

It is one of the great paradoxes of the age. Science feeds a growing belief in inevitable human progress, is the great motivating force of the seemingly boundless optimism and confidence of the Victorian era; and yet, its very success threatens the basis of man's self-esteem as a being created by God in his own image. Mary Shelley's *Frankenstein* (1818) strikingly enacts the dangerous but exciting paradox: man, who through the discoveries of science seems more and more able to manipulate the creation itself, does so by unleashing forces which render him passive and vulnerable in a mechanistic cosmos now robbed of ultimate meaning. Thomas Carlyle's description of the spiritual collapse of Teufelsdröckh, in his widely read *Sartor Resartus* (1839), must have reflected the confused feelings of many Victorians:

> Some comfort it would have been, could I, like a Faust, have fancied myself tempted and tormented of the Devil; for a Hell, as I imagine, without Life, though only diabolic Life, were more frightful: but in our age of Down-pulling and Disbelief, the very Devil has been pulled down, you cannot so much as believe in a Devil. To me the Universe was all void of Life, of Purpose, of Volition, even of Hostility: it was one huge, dead, immeasurable Steam-engine, rolling on in its dead indifference, to grind me limb from limb. Oh, the vast, gloomy, solitary Golgotha, and Mill of Death![31]

One result of this disorientation was to drive those who suffered from it (and in a number of ways it was a phenomenon which deeply affected many) onwards to the hoped-for serenity of a world in which man would be supreme. It was precisely the new and exciting sense of autonomous human power which had, paradoxically, led him to a kind of base camp where he felt naked and afraid, a place from which were poignantly visible the old certainties and where the old resonances, haunting but no longer reassuring, lingered in the memory. Before him, though, still rose the peak on which man would be both autonomous and secure; a peak yet to be conquered, but one where the old need for ultimate value, whose persistence had, partly at least, imprisoned him within his present divided condition, would itself be exorcized.

THE MARGINALIZATION OF GOD

Just as many people, of course, underwent no such tribulations. The optimism of the period was as characteristic as its doubts. Not a few took to the new world in which man and man alone was to be captain of his own soul without a backward glance. Samuel Smiles's dictum, 'the world is his, who has patience and industry',[32] might almost be a motto for the century itself; more and more, man was to see himself as self-made; as though irresistibly, he increasingly saw himself rather than God at the centre. The reasons for this are many, and the ground had been long prepared. One strand in a complex story, clearly enough, is one Enlightenment belief: that man is born in a state of original innocence, and that human societies, therefore, need only to establish themselves on rational principles for all human problems to melt away. 'The damage', pronounced Jacob Burckhardt in 1871 (referring to the 'disgusting optimism' of the bourgeoisie), 'was begun in the last century, mainly through Rousseau, with his doctrine of the goodness of human nature. Out of this plebs and educated alike distilled the doctrine of the golden age that was to come quite infallibly, provided people were left alone.'[33]

But Rousseau's was not the only Enlightenment doctrine of man, nor is the 'Enlightenment' itself quite so easy to fathom. Optimism, 'disgusting' or not, is not the only attitude associated with the belief that (in the words of Alexander Pope) it was '*The* business of Man not to pry into *God*, but to study *himself*'.[34] The famous lines from *An Essay on Man* (1736) which these words summarize indicate that man's increasing self-absorption has as much to do with his uncertainties as with any growth of confidence in his innate virtue or abilities:

> Know then thyself, presume not God to scan;
> The proper study of Mankind is Man.
> Placed on this isthmus of a middle state,

> A Being darkly wise, and rudely great:
> With too much knowledge for the Sceptic side,
> With too much weakness for the Stoic's pride,
> He hangs between; in doubt to act, or rest;
> In doubt to deem himself a God, or Beast. . .[35]

But however we perceive its origins, it is a crucial observation for our inquiry that this movement towards an anthropocentrically perceived culture (which we can see gathering momentum during the eighteenth century, but which does not, as it were, reach 'critical mass' until the nineteenth) is a process which now has all the *appearance* – illusory or not – of being inevitable, so that in essentials it could have taken place *in no other way than the way it did*. So much is this the case, that it seems almost eccentric to mention the fact, let alone to ask seriously whether mankind's post-Enlightenment awareness of itself was, in the generally agreed version, the only one which could have made sense of the world as it now appeared to be. And this apparent inevitability is a phenomenon which has a significance of its own: it is as though the shift from a God-centred to a Man-centred culture were somehow part of the nature of things; we might almost say that being seen as inevitable, the cultural history of Western Man as it has actually unfolded now partakes of the kind of unanswerable authority formerly accorded to divine revelation.

It is hardly possible to overestimate the significance of this development for faith. Human culture has become the measure of all things in a way totally unimaginable for previous ages. And this has become seen less as an historical development to be assessed by theology, than as one by which theology itself is to be judged. Man's new and ambiguous stature, the greater autonomy which has come, willy nilly, from having to live in a cosmos apparently now barren of supernatural activity, have become habits of mind, for Christians and secular humanists alike. And for some theologians, this has resulted in a more or less explicitly expressed understanding that theology now finds itself in a definitively changed cultural and historical situation, for which the activity of God is marginal. This is Don Cupitt's historical understanding of the condition of Western Man, one which all authentic theology must in his view now reflect:

> As ideas of meaning and value were withdrawn from nature they
> became concentrated within the human realm, and Western

thinking became steadily more man-centred or anthropocentric. Through critical philosophy and philosophy of language, and through the development of history and the social sciences, it came to be realized how completely we are enclosed within the limits of our own humanity, bound by history, culture and language, and able to see the world only from a human point of view which is itself perpetually shifting. We can have no absolute knowledge, and may count ourselves fortunate if we can justify our claims to some objective knowledge of the world.[36]

Later, he adds the *coup de grâce*:

In effect, the development of critical thinking and of the scientific outlook has now demythologized or demystified all the things that people have traditionally lived by. Religions, ideologies, moralities, and even such basic social institutions as marriage and the nation-state have all been reduced by sceptical analysis to complex cultural transforms and masks of the raw biological will to power.[37]

DEMYTHOLOGIZING THE DEMYTHOLOGIZERS

Two observations need to be made about this understanding. The first is that, though Cupitt himself occupies a theological position so radical that it is now difficult to see why he continues to call himself a Christian at all, his general posture is in some important respects that of many theologians who are apparently far from accepting what is for him the natural outcome of this marginalization of the Christian creator-God: that is, the actual denial of his objective reality. Cupitt's refusal to contemplate seriously the idea of a God who effectively intervenes in the lives of men and women, and his emphasis on religion as providing, rather, a subjective personal resource, 'a body of ideals and practices that have the power to give ultimate worth to human life', is shared, for instance, by Maurice Wiles, despite Wiles's relatively traditional belief in a creator-God with overall responsibility for having set the creation going in the first place. Hence, Wiles tells us that 'man's imaginative and active faculties can be expanded by the vision of God' (a phrase not to be taken in any objective sense) 'in ways that continue to excite and surprise us'. 'But', he goes on, 'when we speak of particular occasions – whether the inspiration of Scripture, a eucharistic service, the history of the Church, the lives of the saints, or even special experiences of our own – as scenes of the Holy Spirit's activity, we need not (*indeed, I would be bold enough to say we ought not*) imply thereby that they are occasions in which some special supernatural causation is to be looked for.'[38] There *is* a divine purpose; but it is on our autonomous response to that purpose that its effective realization must wholly rely.

The apprehension that divine activity has, for all practical purposes, been withdrawn from the cosmos is, in this view, one inescapable effect of modern knowledge: now, willy nilly, we must try to conform with his purposes under our own strength, and guided by our own understanding, which is in its turn based on evidence possessing a sound and therefore *recent* pedigree. 'We who inherit the consequences of the enlightenment', writes Dennis Nineham with stoic grandeur, 'cannot with integrity divest ourselves of our autonomy. However much help we get from the Bible, however reluctantly we may part company with it . . . we must . . . *decide for ourselves*, with the help of such light as we can get, what our stance before God, and our attitude to our neighbour, should be.'[39] The truth has not been given by God; it is our business to find it.

This brings us to our second observation on Cupitt's general historical assumption about the revolution in human perceptions which has, during the course of the last century and a half, come – apparently irresistibly – to exercise an ever-growing influence over theological speculation: the supposition, that is, that 'the development of critical thinking and of the scientific outlook has now demythologized or demystified all the things that people have traditionally lived by'.[40] The simple fact is that this assumption is itself now widely seen to be in need of a generous measure of demythologization and demystification. 'This task is made considerably easier by the discovery that the criteria for such a demythologization are to be found within the canons of the "critical thinking" itself, in its central tenet that we are wholly "enclosed within the limits of our own humanity, bound by history, culture and language, and able to see the world only from a human point of view which is itself perpetually shifting".'[41] Sooner or later, the discovery was inevitable that the critical revolution is itself a prime example of the culture-bound vision it attributes to almost every belief on which it has assumed (from a perspective claimed to be 'scientific') a competence to offer impartial and definitive judgement.

22

Nowhere has the development of this 'critical' thinking had a more revolutionary outcome for Christianity than in its connection with the way in which the biblical texts themselves have become marginal for theology, and a problem for Christian men and women in the exercise of their faith; and nowhere is the need for the demystifiers to be themselves coolly assessed more pressing. There are, in fact, already clear signs that scholars are beginning to address themselves to the problems faced by the Church as the result of allowing biblical scholarship (and therefore theology) to become dominated by a critical perspective the procedures and philosophical origins of which have been largely unexamined. 'We may recognize', as Henning Graf von Reventlow puts it in his magisterial work *The Authority of the Bible and the Rise of the Modern World* (1979), 'that one of the most important reasons for the vanishing role of biblical study in the wider context of theology is a failure of exegetes to reflect adequately on their methodology and the presuppositions, shaped by their view of the world, which they bring to their work'. Although an intense and extended discussion on hermeneutics has been carried on until the present day, nevertheless, continues von Reventlow,

> for the most part this discussion moved in the realms of esoteric theological reflections, to some degree forming a 'superstructure' to the tacitly accepted foundation of an exegesis which has been taken to be 'historical-critical' and therefore scientific. Reflection on the presuppositions of historical criticism appears only by way of exception ... As soon as that happens, however, it immediately becomes clear that this method cannot be detached from a quite specific understanding of the world and of reality. Only a few years ago it was possible simply to identify the view of the world thus defined with modern thought. Now, however, when we can see the intrinsic fragility of these presuppositions ... it is desirable that we should dig deeper and uncover the ideological and social roots to which more recent biblical criticism owes its origin, its deeper impetus and the direction of the answers which it gives.[42]

THE NEW INFALLIBILITY

Two effects of the dominance of what has become known as 'the higher

23

criticism' may be noted in passing. The first derives from what can only be described as its inbuilt élitist tendency. As Bishop Lesslie Newbigin rightly observes, 'many Christians feel themselves to be in a position analogous to that which was a ground of complaint at the time of the Reformation. At that time the complaint was that the Bible had been taken out of the hands of the laity and become the property of the clergy. Now it has to be asked whether it has not become the property of the guild of scholars in such a way that the ordinary layman feels unable to understand it without the help of a trained expert.' We need to add, though, that it is not only by the complexity (not to mention the massive volume) of modern critical scholarship that the Bible has been taken out of the hands of the laity; more important perhaps, is the way in which criticism has steadily eroded the authority of Scripture as truly embodying the self-revelation of God, so that for generation after generation of Christian men and women, the Bible has become less and less central to the teaching they receive from their pastors as a means of actually *knowing* about God. They may never hear about biblical criticism from the pulpit; its effect on preaching and catechetics has nevertheless been immense. It is also clearly a principal contributory cause of the gulf, frequently remarked, between modern theologians and ordinary Christians.

Another result of the dominance of the higher criticism, a result which derives largely from the fact that its presuppositions are, as Reventlow suggests, 'tacitly accepted', and its exegesis generally taken to be 'scientific', is that it is very difficult to question it without attracting accusations of obscurantism. Such accusations need not be in the form of any obviously detectable, or intended, imputation of intellectual deviance; nor are the defenders of the current conventional wisdom anything but consciously persuaded of the desirability of theological 'pluralism'. Nevertheless, there is no question but that they are as profoundly convinced of the infallible character of their own intellectual presuppositions as the most bigoted fundamentalist. Their means of inducing belief in their own assumptions are certainly not generally consciously intended as such; they are nevertheless powerful, and generally effective. Normally implicitly, though sometimes quite explicitly, doubters are confronted by the accepted orthodoxy on recent intellectual history. The spectral vision of Galileo before the Inquisition tends somehow to rise hauntingly to the mind's eye, with the higher criticism cast as Copernican astronomy (irreversible intellectual breakthrough) and those sceptical of its claims represented as the Inquisition (tired and intellectually bankrupt tradition resisting fresh thinking because incapable of coping with change). Few seminarians are equipped to challenge such a view, however deep their instinct that there is something badly wrong with it; nor will theology undergraduates in many, perhaps most, universities in Britain and North America receive help or encouragement from their teachers to ask searching questions about the actual basis of the received view, whose presuppositions they are expected tacitly to accept and perpetuate.

The view that a Man-centred culture (in which the non-intervention of God is taken as axiomatic) should now be the source of the guiding assumptions of theology and biblical criticism is, as we have seen, widely assumed to be one inevitable outcome of the scientific revolution of the last two centuries. Since science and the Christian tradition are now supposed to be incompatible; since science is 'real and verifiable' knowledge, and the biblical record 'is not'; since it is now believed that man has no source of real understanding of himself and his place in the universe but that alone which results from his unaided observation and reason; it follows then, as night follows day, that a revolution in the way we do theology – one in which the perceptual shift from a God-centred to a Man-centred cosmos is precisely mirrored – is the only way in which Christianity can reestablish its relevance for the human culture in which it must now operate.

To say that this revolution is well under way (many would say very nearly achieved in some Western countries) is to explain what is meant here by saying that the Church is already, or is becoming, *secularized*; to say that it is at least open to question whether the entire analysis on which the revolution is based may be substantially, perhaps entirely, misconceived, is to suggest that it may be time for the Church to be *desecularized*, together with many of the assumptions from which its secularization originally proceeded. It may be, not only that this time has come, but that the process is actually under way. It may also be that, although the influence of 'critical thinking' on biblical scholarship and theology has been immense, it has acted on the life of the Church more by sapping the spiritual authority of its public representatives than by really changing the beliefs of ordinary Christian people. Hence, though the need for the revitalization of theology is certainly urgent, the effects of secularization have been partly contained by the remoteness of its proponents from the real lives of ordinary Christians in the parish; the process of *desecularization*, therefore, could well be easier than might have been predicted: something like a palace revolution (or, more accurately, counter-revolution) perhaps helped along by a certain element of popular revolt.

BISHOP JENKINS (1): CHRISTIAN DOCTRINE

This last suggestion may be less whimsical than at first appears. The gulf between 'critical' theology and most normal Christians, and the way in which this theology tends to be decisively rejected 'on the ground' *when it actually begins to impinge on the Church as a community of faith* (having emerged from the academic haunts where it may normally be safely ignored), was dramatically illustrated in 1984 in the so-called 'Jenkins affair'. Professor David Jenkins, having been nominated to the prestigious bishopric of Durham, appeared on Thames Television's *Credo* programme, and made it clear that he did not believe in either the virgin conception of Christ or in his bodily resurrection; he did, he claimed, believe in the resurrection itself, though not as an historical event. These were, and remained, distinctions which for nearly everyone were wholly incomprehensible. A petition to the Archbishop of York against his consecration as bishop attracted over 14,000 signatures in five weeks. This the archbishop rejected with the pronouncement, before television news cameras, that 'some people are so gullible, they will sign anything'.

More, however, was displayed than the entire remoteness (even élitism) of the liberal theological establishment, though this is certainly not the least of the lessons of this extraordinary episode (one abiding memory of the affair is the apparent astonishment of Professor Jenkins himself who, not without reason, pointed out that he had said nothing he had not said many times before; nothing, indeed, which had not been a theological commonplace for over a century). What may prove to be of greater significance in the end was the emergence of what Professor John Macquarrie, in his book *The Faith of the People of God*, has called 'the people as primary theological datum':[43] one is almost tempted to recall (from a very different context) the words of Origen: 'something new has happened . . . the massive rise of the Christian people, as if suddenly brought forth'.[44]

For what was to be observed was not only an urgent demand that it be recognized that the faith of the people of God was their heritage rather than the intellectual property of the professional theologians; what manifested itself was a great public declaration about the nature of that faith and of the Christian community itself, and it was a declaration which, largely unconsciously, constituted a direct challenge to the prevailing theological consensus. The declaration about faith was that, though it might be conceded that (in Dr Macquarrie's words) 'faith is more than belief', even that 'revelation is more than knowledge',[45] *belief and knowledge nevertheless precede faith and not the other way round*; or as Newman would have put it, 'notional assent' comes before 'real assent'. The declaration about the Christian community itself was that a commonly held body of belief and of knowledge is the foundation of a common faith, to the maintenance and propagation of which certain members of the community are specially called. The people of God were doing what they had so often been urged to do: they were 'participating' in '*doing* theology'; and they were being massively snubbed for their pains.

BISHOP JENKINS (2): SOCIAL THEOLOGY

The 'Jenkins affair' focused attention, not only on fundamental issues of faith and doctrine, but also on another area of difficulty for the modern Church, one in which Dr Jenkins's pronouncements (once his notoriety had been established) were to receive even greater attention from the news media. Both before and after his consecration as bishop, he now issued a series of pronouncements on political and social issues, generally hostile to the Conservative government then in power, and given wide currency by the hostile reaction of the administration itself. These contained little which had not been heard from the Church of England's official and semi-official spokesmen (whether members of the bench of bishops or the Board for Social Responsibility) many times before; but they served to bring to the public consciousness once again the vexed question of 'religion and politics'. This time, however, there was an added dimension to the debate: a new question began to be asked. The issue, previously, had tended to revolve around such questions as 'should the Church keep out of politics?' or (less crudely) some such speculation as this: 'Since Christianity is an ethical religion, and since therefore there can be no question of the Church wholly *withdrawing* from comment on social and political issues, how do we distinguish between – on the one hand – what is legitimate comment on matters of fundamental principle and – on the other – illegitimate involvement in ephemeral and detailed judgements about how those principles ought to be applied in particular situations?'

Now, a new question was asked, by some at least; though whether any very satisfactory answer was generally forthcoming may be doubted. Dr Jenkins had become notorious for his denial of certain doctrines, and had clearly identified his denials with a particular attitude to theology, with that 'development of critical thinking and of the scientific outlook' which, according to the logically consistent Don Cupitt, 'has now demythologized or demystified all the things that people have traditionally lived by'.[46] Having proclaimed himself a demystifier, Dr Jenkins issued a series of statements on political and social questions which were generally understood as being left-wing, even Marxist in tone and intention. Was there, some asked, any underlying connection between his theology and his politics? To this, the answer was generally 'no', if for no other reason than that there was an established alternative tradition linking orthodox theology and socialism; there had even been a link (in Germany during the 1930s) between liberal theology and Nazism. Such connections were invalid; Dr Jenkins's theological and political views were seen as related only by a personal tendency to iconoclasm.

The question, perhaps, had been asked in the wrong way; for it remained clear that the political Jenkins and the theological Jenkins were part of the same phenomenon, and that this phenomenon was more than merely personal. First, because Dr Jenkins was far more representative both of the politics *and* the theology of the leadership of the Church than was at first realized; secondly, because it was obvious that there must be *some* intellectual link between these two aspects of Dr Jenkins's consciousness more essential than his obvious relish for making mischief. But the essential link was not discoverable in the quite distinct 'radicalisms' of his political and his theological views: it was, on the contrary, to be found – a very different matter – in their common *secularism*. The necessary link was between an anthropocentric theology and a wholly secular view of social and political life: a marginalized and non-interventionist God left no alternative but to centre both theology and politics on Man himself; the function of 'God' here being to act as a kind of rhetorical device, a personification of the current progressive idealism favoured by the writer. As Eric Mascall had written some twenty years before, of an earlier generation of demythologizers (before pointing to the influence of Bultmann on the secularisms of the 1960s):

> Not the least weakness of this type of radical secularization is that it entirely undermines the whole notion of Christian social theology; just because it completely capitulates to the outlook of the contemporary world it has no criterion for passing judgement on it. It has no *pou sto* from which to move the world; and the whole of that great tradition of social thought which was revived [in the Church of England] by F. D. Maurice, and which produced such great figures as Gore, Temple, and Widdrington is deprived of all ground and justification.[47]

Here lies the key, perhaps, for an understanding, not of the 'Jenkins affair' only, but of much else in the life of the contemporary Western Church; most obviously, perhaps, for an understanding of why the increasing frequency of its pronouncements on social and political affairs has not led to any corresponding growth of acceptance by the world at large that the Church really *has* a distinctive contribution to make in this area, a contribution which is not available from any other source.

PROPHECY IN A POST-MODERN AGE

It is, nevertheless, important to understand that more is at stake here than the renewal of a capacity within the Church for doing an authentically Christian social theology, important though that un-doubtedly is. What is truly at stake is the renewal of *all* Christian theology, the recovery for the Church of a theology which is truly *prophetic*. And the word 'prophetic' is used in this context deliberately, so that it may be reclaimed for its proper use, to indicate not the proclamation of one human philosophy against another (with or without a rhetorical admixture of biblical language), but the absolute judgement of a God-centred perspective on *all* Man-centred philo-sophies or ideologies. The Church needs once more to be able to say, with Paul, that its teaching is 'not a wisdom of this age or of the rulers of this age, who are doomed to pass away'; and that its faith rests 'not . . . in the wisdom of men but in the power of God' (1 Cor. 2.6,5). The prophet was pre-eminently the man set apart to press deep into the burning and mysterious vastness of the desert, there to commune with God; and on his return to the fallen and tangled complexity of the city, to recall the people to their obedience to that immense reality. Idolatry was seen above all as the setting-up of a human and imaginable reality as the object of that ultimate commitment due alone to the mystery of God himself.

It is the conviction of the authors of this book that the time has come in which it is not only possible but essential to regain such a prophetic theology, not as a regressive assertion of old intellectual formulations, but as a discovery (which will be itself in one vital way a new one) of how the Christian revelation, the 'deposit of faith' given by God, always dynamic, unchanging in its essence, endless in its implications for every conceivable human culture and historical circumstance, will transform human understanding of the new age into which civilization is now moving. It will, without doubt, be an age in which an authentically Christian perspective will be needed as urgently as at any time during the 'modern period'. It was the very essence of the 'modern' vision that we had reached an understanding against which all former understanding could be judged. 'Modern' knowledge was definitive; mankind had come of age. Now, this understanding is crumbling; increasingly we can see (to use Reventlow's expression) the 'intrinsic fragility' of the presuppositions on which it was built.

We are moving into what some writers are now calling a 'post-modern' period, and it could be one of intense and growing uncertainty, even despair, unless we begin now to scrutinize the beliefs and assumptions about Man, about human civilization, above all about God himself, which have brought us to our present condition. For the Church, such a scrutiny is the indispensable first stage towards an understanding that (to quote the partially reconstructed Harvey Cox once more) 'with the passing of the modern age, the epoch of "modern theology" which tried to interpret Christianity in the face of secularization is also over. A fundamentally new approach is needed.'[48]

So much is increasingly clear: what needs to be added is that nothing is more vital for the viability of any such approach than a clear perception that it is not those *defending* a revealed Christianity who are the representatives of an exhausted and dying culture; it is, on the contrary, those who present what they understand as 'the Enlightenment legacy' or 'the assured results of modern knowledge', as a definitive –

or at least, the only available – guide into the uncertainties of the third millenium.

It is a message which waits vainly to be heard by those who still guard the conventional wisdom of mainline liberal secularist Christendom. Hence, for example, when – in the aftermath of the 'Jenkins affair' – the Anglican priest David Holloway reaffirmed the biblical revelation in his book *The Church of England: Where is it Going?* (1985), his arguments were loftily dismissed by the reviewer, the Very Revd David L. Edwards, as 'innocent'. David Holloway's reply, published under the title 'An Open Letter to a Champion of Theological Liberalism', effectively made clear not only the reviewer's personal bias, but also his remoteness from reality. As Holloway points out, his review entirely failed even to touch on the book's argument that 'we are living in a post-Enlightenment world in the West'. 'So many liberal protestants', Holloway tellingly continues,

> seem to me to be inhabiting (intellectually) not *that* world, but rather a ghost world long past. Some, indeed, are intellectually still locked into the 'Sixties' (the period when you were at the SCM Press and published *Honest to God*). Thus there is a liberal form of 'fundamentalism'. It is an inability to escape from a fixed 'belief in Science (with a capital 'S').[49]

YESTERDAY'S MEN

It is the greatest irony of all; those who have assumed the mantle of Galileo now close ranks to defend a world-view more and more seen as cloistered and obscurantist. Those like Bishop Jenkins who truly believe that it is their mission in life to drag the Church into line with the implications for theology of what they suppose to be 'modern knowledge' ('modern' in the sense of being current), are in truth yesterday's men, 'intellectually still locked into the 1960s', into a period, that is, whose theological suppositions were derived (as we shall see) from Victorian and early-twentieth-century assumptions and attitudes which in every other field of inquiry were even then either crumbling or long since obsolete.

It needs to be said, of course, that no civilization simply collapses overnight; nor are the assumptions of the old culture ever wholly replaced by those of the new. If we return to Polanyi's indispensable comparison between our own age and that of St Augustine, we find there no warrant for an entire *rejection* of the 'legacy of the Enlightenment' (an entity which, as Dr Hankey's essay indicates, must in any case be evoked in this context with more caution than it often is). Certainly, we can speak of Augustine as standing at the end of one culture and at the beginning of a new one. But the new dispensation which Augustine represents, though it inaugurates in one way a radical departure from the decaying classical culture of the time, can be seen in another way as the vehicle by which that culture's achievements were continued into the new age. It was above all through the influence of Augustine that neo-Platonism was to dominate Christian philosophy until the thirteenth century and beyond.

It was not in a replacement of Classical thought by something quite unconnected with it that Augustine's achievement lay. Classical reason was to be used, not cast down. But it was to be made subject to the authority of the Christian revelation. The reason of the philosophers had its own authority, was, indeed, only possible by divine gift. Nevertheless, it could not by itself give the meaning of human life: that could be imparted only by special revelation, by God's own self-disclosure conveyed by Holy Scripture. 'Understanding is the reward of faith', said Augustine; 'therefore do not seek to understand in order to believe, but believe in order that you may understand; for unless you believe, you will not understand' (*Joan. Evang.*, xxix.6). Faith becomes now a means of understanding, without which the achievements of autonomous human reason are void. It is this fundamental and revolutionary Christian perception that liberal modernist Christian thinking has precisely reversed, and which any post-modern theology will have to restore as a basic condition of viability.

Time after time down the Christian centuries, the Church has found renewal at times of its own confusion or decadence in a return to the person of Christ. This has been possible, because no matter how much the Church's leaders may in any age have lost their own authority as teachers of the faith, the risen Christ himself was still accessible – in a number of ways, but crucially through the gospel record and the apostolic teachings, particularly those of Paul. The authority of Scripture has never been in any serious doubt until the present age: the first priority, therefore, for any serious attempt to move beyond our present failed theologies must be to understand how this loss of authority could have occurred, and whether it is possible with intellectual integrity to reverse it.

Hence the first, as well as the longest, essay in this book consists of a serious examination of the philosophical presuppositions of the biblical criticism of the last century and a half. For as Professor Hankey puts it, 'The ideas the critic brings to the text are . . . crucial. If he is able to think in the way that those who wrote the text thought, he will be successful and make right judgements about it. On the other hand, if the scholar imports ideas far distant from the logic informing the text, the opposite will result. The intellectual assumptions of the scholar will be all important.'[50] His conclusions are clear: not only that 'the philosophical and theological presuppositions determining the methods and conclusions of higher biblical criticism are questionably appropriate to the biblical text', but that 'this was well-known to those who began the higher criticism of Scripture';[51] as Hankey shows, the declared aim of this approach 'is to separate the Scripture from the Church and its doctrine, which claims to derive from Scripture and reciprocally to be that through which Scripture can be intelligible'. It is vital to assert, however, that '*this reciprocity is necessary if both Scripture and Church are the work of the Holy Spirit*' (my emphasis).[52]

If it is indeed possible (as we conclude) to move beyond the scepticism about biblical authority which has characterized much, if not most, modernist and liberal theology, the question then arises: what are the biblical teachings on the relationship between man and God (between – on the one hand – human understanding and self-will and – on the other – God's own self-disclosure and will for his creation) which will form the necessary background to any new theology which will be authentically 'prophetic' in the sense we have indicated here? This is among the questions asked in the second essay, which together with the first forms the opening section of the book entitled 'Recovering the Authority of Scripture'.

FACING THE ISSUES

The title of the book's second part ('Recovering the Authority of God'), indicates that the process of returning to a traditional understanding of revelation cannot be a means of legitimizing a ghetto theology – one, that is, in which human understanding is actually *denied*. Theology was called the 'Queen of the Sciences', not because it had some kind of crude primacy of prestige among other branches of knowledge, but because in a God-centred cosmos it was obvious that only through a theological perspective could the real meaning of *any* knowledge ultimately be plumbed. *Deus scientiarum Dominus*: or, in free translation, God has authority over human knowledge; one might pertinently add 'and not the other way round'.

For if one thing is surely becoming increasingly clear, it is that 'modern' theology's increasingly perceived irrelevance is largely due to its subordination of revealed knowledge to a body of preconceptions initially believed to be stable and definitive ('scientific') but now more and more known to be ephemeral, unstable and value-laden, deployed by theologians normally unfamiliar with current work in fields of study on whose now-discarded assumptions they still rely with undiminished confidence. Thus, it was the core of Dr David Jenkins's defence that 'facing the issues of critical study, historical knowledge and scientific thinking is essential';[53] but it did not occur to him that this procedure might now produce very different conclusions from his own; that he is not necessarily, on foundations such as these, any longer (if ever he was) entitled to pronounce: '*Causa finita est*'.

Is it really the case, for instance, that science has disproved the possibility, or even the likelihood, of miraculous intervention in human affairs? Is it *true* that in a scientific age man can be seen to be simply part of nature, to be 'marginal in the cosmos'? *Has* 'the development of . . . the scientific outlook . . . now demythologized or demystified all the things that people have traditionally lived by'? More specifially, has science shown itself to be radically inconsistent with traditional Christian belief? These are among the questions approached by a scientist in chapter three, crucially for our inquiry: for it is on the assumption that there can only be an affirmative answer to such questions that much of what we have called 'secularist' theology rests: answer 'no' and the entire structure begins to show the effects of mining subsidence.

Again, we now need to ask: is it actually *true* that 'historical knowledge' strengthens the secularist case? Does it, for instance, destroy belief in the substantial accuracy of the New Testament record? It is certainly one of the assumptions of modernist theologies that it does. Here, there is an obvious rejoinder: that ancient historians – as Eric Mascall was pointing out twenty years ago – fail to support the 'extreme scepticism about the reliability of their material which is manifested by many New Testament scholars'. Dr Mascall goes on to comment on this 'deeply rooted tendency' to approach biblical material 'in a mood of quite exaggerated scepticism', that

> This may be due to a laudable desire to attract the outsider to the Church by persuading him that it is possible to be a Christian on the basis of a much smaller body of reliable factual material than has generally been supposed to be necessary; I suspect that his usual reaction is a decision that if the factual basis of Christianity is so limited and precarious he might just as well stay where he is, and a suspicion – no doubt quite unjustified – that the biblical theologians would themselves abandon the formal profession of Christianity if they had not a vested interest in its propagation.[54]

But facing the issue of historical knowledge may be done also in a quite different way; for we may now begin to look dispassionately, not only at the history of the Church in the first century, but at its history during the nineteenth and twentieth centuries: and specifically at how the secularization of society has been mirrored within the Church, above all in its absorption of distinctively secular values, 'secular' here in the quite particular sense that they can be specially identified with the *saeculum*, the age, in which they have their origin and greatest influence. In chapter four, an ecclesiastical historian of the period examines certain ways in which this process can be seen to have taken place, and asks whether or not it has actually increased the Church's attractiveness to the surrounding culture; whether, indeed, the ideals and motives thus absorbed from the secular world are ones which have any natural affinity or even consistency with the Christian religion.

Our conclusions here are crucial for the kind of answer we give to the question with which we began: Bonhoeffer's inquiry as to 'what Christianity really is, or indeed who Christ really is, for us today'. For we will never find out who Christ is for us, today or at any time, by looking into a mirror at what we hope is our most altruistic face; or what Christianity is, by – in effect – reading off from the surrounding culture its most apparently progressive and humanitarian tendencies. Such tendencies may well be not only consistent with Christianity, but also derived from Christian influences: but this cannot be *assumed*; nor, even when it can, does this necessarily provide us with a basis for understanding how Christianity is to be made (or rather *shown to be*) relevant to a modern urban culture.

Nowhere is this perception more needed than in the whole area of Christian social concern: it is above all else the widespread belief that many of the Churches' recent political and social involvements have had no discernibly Christian content, that has led to (surely unacceptable) demands for the Church not to concern itself with such matters in any way at all. Hence the last chapter of this book, by a former chairman of the Church of England's Board for Social Responsibility, deals with the 'Desecularization of the Social Gospel': with the restoration, that is, of the perception that all social theology must have at its root the knowledge that the ultimate social problem is man's estrangement from God, and that one inescapable consequence of this is his alienation from his neighbour.

The basis of the renewal of social theology, therefore, is the same as the basis of the Christian life itself: it has to do with the regaining of that divine hunger for life in the presence of God which is at the root of all other human longing, whether we have recognized it for what it is or not. It is belief in what Austin Farrer calls 'this infinite and invaluable gift, this partaking of God's eternity' which, as he says, is 'the acid test of genuine faith'. For, as Farrer continues,

> Leave this out of account, and you can equivocate for ever on God's very existence: your talk about God can always be talk about the backside of nature, dressed in emotional rhetoric. But a God who reverses nature, a God who undoes death, that those in whom the likeness of his glory has faintly and fitfully shone may be drawn everlastingly into the heart of light, and know him as he is: this is a God indeed, a God Almighty, a God to be trusted, loved, adored.[55]

NOTES

1   Cited in S. Sykes, *The Integrity of Anglicanism* (London 1979), p. 9.
2   BBC Radio 4 Series, Lent 1986, 'The Turn of the Tide'.
3   M. Muggeridge, *Something Beautiful for God* (London 1972), p. 56.
4   *Church Times*, 14 February 1986.
5   Ibid.
6   Muggeridge, op. cit., pp. 31–2.
7   *Daily Telegraph*, 24 December 1985.
8   Ibid.

9   See L. Newbigin, *The Other Side of 84* (London 1983), p. 1.
10 J. L. Russell, 'The Religion of Progress', *Scrutiny*, III (1934–5), pp. 268–82.
11 Newbigin, op. cit., pp. 25–6.
12 H. Cox, *The Secular City* (London 1965), p. 4.
13 J. Bowden, and J. Richmond (eds.), *A Reader in Contemporary Theology* (London 1967), p. 90.
14 Ibid.
15 Cox, op. cit., p. 4.
16 H. Cox, *Religion in the Secular City* (New York 1984), p. 20.
17 Bowden and Richmond, op. cit.
18 See B. Häring, *Faith and Morality in a Secular Age*, (London 1973), pp. 1–20.
19 *The Secular City*, op. cit., p. 2.
20 E. Mascall, *The Secularisation of Christianity* (London 1965), pp. 190–91.
21 D. Jenkins, *Guide to the Debate about God* (London 1966), p. 97.
22 J. H. Newman, *Parochial and Plain Sermons*, vol. VII, sermon iii.
23 Ibid.
24 C. A. Watts, *The Meaning of Rationalism* (London 1905).
25 O. Chadwick, *The Secularization of the European Mind in the Nineteenth Century* (Cambridge 1975), pp. 162–3.
26 D. Cupitt, *The World to Come* (London 1982), p. ix.
27 B. Russell, *Mysticism and Logic* (London 1928), pp. 47–8.
28 H. P. Liddon, *Some Elements of Religion* (London 1872), p. 56.
29 M. C. Church, *The Life and Letters of Dean Church* (London 1985), p. 153.
30 G. J. Romanes, *A Candid Examination of Theism* (London 1878), p. 114.
31 T. Carlyle, *Sartor Resartus* (Boston 1884), p. 126.
32 S. Smiles, *Self-Help* (London 1859).
33 Alexander Dru (ed.), *The Letters of Jacob Burckhardt*, (London 1955), 2 July 1871.
34 J. Bailey (ed.), *Poems of Alexander Pope* (London 1947), p. 125.
35 Ibid.
36 Cupitt, op. cit., pp. viii–ix.
37 Ibid., p. xv.
38 M. Wiles, *The Remaking of Christian Doctrine* (London 1974), pp. 101–2.
39 D. Nineham, *The Use and Abuse of the Bible* (London 1976), p. 205.
40 Cupitt, op. cit., p. xv.
41 Ibid., pp. viii–ix.
42 Henning Graf von Reventlow, *The Authority of the Bible and the Rise of the Modern World* (London 1985), pp. 1–2.
43 J. Macquarrie, *The Faith of the People of God* (London 1972), ch. 2.
44 Origen, *Contra Celsum*, VIII.
45 Macquarrie, op. cit., p. 12.
46 Cupitt, op. cit., p. xv.
47 Mascall, op. cit., p. 8.
48 Cox, op. cit., p. 21.
49 *Church Times*, 13 and 20 September, 1985.

50 See p. 47 below.
51 See p. 48 below.
52 See p. 49 below.
53 *Church Times*, 20 September 1985.
54 Mascall, op. cit., p. 215.
55 A. Farrer, *The End of Man* (London 1973), p. 4.

PART ONE
Recovering the Authority of Scripture

1 The Bible in a Post-Critical[1] Age

WAYNE HANKEY

Christian theology is thinking, which is faithful participation in God's self-revelation in the Holy Scriptures of our religion. Those who use the Book of Common Prayer (1662) are reminded on the Fourth Sunday after Trinity of the logic which necessitates the divine revelation recorded in the Holy Scriptures of the Christian Church.[2] 'Can the blind lead the blind?' asks Jesus in the Gospel. 'Shall they not both fall into the ditch?' Our Lord goes on to assert forcefully the blindness of fallen humanity. 'How canst thou say to thy brother, Brother, let me pull out the mote that is in thine eye, when thou thyself beholdest not the beam that is in thine eye?' The Epistle, from St Paul's Letter to the Romans, brings out that the journey we are too blind to lead is the movement of creation from the bondage and pain of corruptibility into the eternal and 'glorious liberty of the children of God', 'the redemption of our bodies'. The Collect teaches that the mercy of God as 'our ruler and guide' is altogether requisite if we are to 'so pass through things temporal that we finally lose not the things eternal'.

WHAT IS REVELATION?

By considering what connects these propers, we discover the characteristic marks of revelation. First, the aim of revelation is to restore our freedom so that as rational beings we might know where we are going and how to get there. We are by revelation given the knowledge of our end and the means to the end so that we may with the rational freedom which belongs to our true original and new redeemed nature direct ourselves towards it. Revelation as the communication of knowledge is addressed to man understood as rational and, because rational, capable of freedom. 'Ye shall know the truth and the truth will make you free' (John 8.32). Secondly, the revelation is thus essentially knowledge, but it is knowledge which restores and redirects

41

the world towards its eternal good. It is primarily theoretical, but it is a theory which includes and embraces the practical. As Thomas Aquinas puts it:

> Sacred Doctrine is both practical and theoretical, just as by a single knowledge God both knows himself and what he does. It is however more theoretical than practical since it is more concerned with the things of God which already exist than with things men do; it deals with human actions so far as by them man is directed towards the complete knowledge God has and in which eternal happiness consists (*Summa Theologiae*, 1.1.4).

Thirdly, the knowledge conveyed is principally and ultimately about the eternal. It comes from an eternity which draws the temporal and physical back into itself. The purpose of this self-revelation of the eternal is that man, knowing his eternal end, might direct himself and grow towards it. Revelation is from eternity and for eternity; it concerns temporal things only as means. It is not immediately or directly a science of the temporal or physical, nor does it aim to teach us to use them except in so far as we may thereby attain eternal life.[3] Scripture does not essentially then contain truth about nature and worldly ends, but it must teach us the changeless truth about eternity and those moral principles by which we may 'so pass through things temporal that we finally lose not the things eternal'. We may sum up this account in the words of Richard Hooker in his *Laws of Ecclesiastical Politie*:

> The end of the word of God is *to save*, and therefore we term it *the word of life*. The way for all men to be saved is by the knowledge of that truth which the word hath taught . . . To this end the word of God no otherwise serveth than only in the nature of a doctrinal instrument. It saveth because it maketh 'wise to salvation'. Wherefore the ignorant it saveth not; they which live by the word must know it . . . sith God, who knoweth and discloseth best the rich treasures of his own wisdom, hath by delivering his word made choice of the Scriptures as the most effectual means whereby those treasures might be imparted unto the world, it followeth that to man's understanding the Scripture must be even of itself intended as a full and perfect discovery, sufficient to imprint in us the lively character of all things

necessarily required for the attainment of eternal life (v, xxi, 3; Keble ii, p. 85).

This teaching concerning the revelation in Scripture is implicit in the Book of Common Prayer and in the 'Articles of the Christian Religion' and is the explicit doctrine of St Thomas Aquinas and of Richard Hooker. It is normative Christian, as well as Anglican, doctrine.

THE MARXIST CONTRAST

This normative doctrine may be usefully understood by contrast with what now represents itself to the Church as a revolutionary new theology and our way forward, and which has an opposed view of the nature and ends of revelation and about how Scripture should be treated. This the so-called contextual, or Marxist theology, theology as praxis. For it, there can be no timeless truth. All theory is relative to the practical context in which it occurs. It is elicited and formed in reflection upon a given historical socio-economic circumstance and the true use of such reflection must be the transformation of that socio-economic reality. The practical embraces the theoretical, rather than the contrary, and man realizes himself in practical activity with respect to the natural and social world: hence, 'praxis' theology.

Praxis must be sharply distinguished from practice. Practice is subordinate to contemplation. The pre-revolutionary Christianity, drawing both on pagan reason and on revelation, taught that man was destined for a self-complete activity beyond the endless doing of things.[4] This self-complete activity is likened to seeing or knowing, because knowledge is a possession of its object. Practice is governed by prudence, since it is presupposed that the end of practice is grasped in knowledge. There is a reasoning which is only calculation about means, but primary and presupposed is a theoretical intuition of the goal of it all. Both for Aristotle and for the Scriptures, this subordination of the practical thus requires that our goal pre-exists in an eternity of which we have some kind of apprehension in this present world.

Praxis replaces practice in the theoretical shift demanded when man is wrenched from his orientation to a transmundane eternal reality. There is then nothing but the endless alternation of calculation and doing. Doing cannot be finally directed to anything beyond itself, and praxis is the new way of designating the practical as endless and essentially purposeless.

That the Scripture should contain truth about eternal things is impossible for theology as praxis. There can be no revelation of an already complete eternity. The idea that man discovers the truth about himself and his world in an eternal heaven apprehended by loving knowledge occurs (according to this contextual theology) because man has not overcome what prevents his attaining his freedom in this world. But the problem arises that this theology is confronted by the existence of the already complete Christian Scripture. The Scriptures must reflect a previous historical socio-economic reality; how, then, are they to be employed in the present activity of theology as praxis? How are they to play a role in reflection on the very different socio-economic reality which confronts us today? How are they to help us to understand our circumstances so that we may change them and in this way bring in the Kingdom of God? The contextual theologian answers:

> Reflection [on] . . . the resources of Scripture and ecclesiastical tradition . . . is informed by reason in the guise of biblical and dogmatic critiques. Just as in the first stage of reflection where reason acts as an open-ended component, always available for revision in the various sciences, so this stage is also open-ended because reason is available for revision here as new biblical and ecclesiastical critiques develop.[5]

The critical biblical scholarship of the last 150 years finds now an explicitly practical, indeed revolutionary, use. It is the means by which the teaching of Scripture is constantly reshaped to make it relevant to the struggles of our time. Modern biblical criticism thus saves the Bible from being either a mere historical document or, what is impossible for praxis, God's Word of eternal life. Critical biblical scholarship constantly reshapes the Scriptures to aid us in the timely transformation of the practical reality surrounding us.

When we began to consider this contextual theology, I hinted that I did not accept its view that it was a new approach and the way forward: this is only its representation of itself. A study of the origins of the critical biblical scholarship of the last 150 years shows that contextual theology has been with us for some time. In fact, it and the Oxford Movement arose together. Dr Pusey went to Germany in the 1820s, and his activity as the Tractarian leader was directed towards saving the Church of England from this 'rationalism'.[6]

It is now common knowledge that the Tractarian reaction against humanistic rationalism as well as the kind of response represented by the first Vatican Council and Pope Leo XIII's Thomistic revival are spent forces.[7] Recent Roman Catholic enthusiasm for the novelties of biblical criticism and Marxist theology has obscured the intellectual difficulties of what these reactions opposed. It is my aim to sketch the character and theological presuppositions of the forms of biblical criticism which arose in the last century. The purpose is to show why, outside certain Liberal Protestant, Roman Catholic and Liberation Theology circles, there is a crisis in biblical criticism. The problem of relating theology and the Bible, treated according to the critical methods which have developed from the nineteenth century, is so acute as to make it impossibly difficult to see how to go on in the same way. Finding the place for these critical methods is now the problem not just for the Churches but 'scientifically'.[8] It is hoped that this exploration of the relation between biblical criticism and theology will also expose some difficulties of Liberation Theology. My purpose here is to show that contextual theology is not the way forward but the decadent tail-end of a dying revolt. The biblical criticism it assumes no longer commands the allegiance of the self-aware leaders of scriptural scholarship. Theology as praxis can now only have as its basis wilful self-assertion and the determination to refashion the Christian religion in the image of that self-assertion. Finally, we shall consider in what sense a solution and way forward is to be found in what preceded the nineteenth-century revolution and the reaction to it.

THE PRESUPPOSITIONS OF CRITICISM

Let us start with a word about the nature and forms of the critical treatment of texts. Any student of classical texts will be aware of how closely related are an interpreter's understanding of the content of a work and the suggestions he makes about doubtful readings of the text – both about what is doubtful and what ought to be done about the problematic passages or words. Put another way, what a scholar is often saying when he appears to be merely discussing grammar is something like: 'From my understanding of what this author teaches, a view formed by my notions of what can be or ought to be taught and thought, I know that he cannot be saying this, he means rather to say that.' This relation between the reader's prior understanding and his

45

intuition that he is reading the text rightly is called the hermeneutic circle. Interpretation is circular because, though understanding is informed by whatever is given in the text before the reader, he never escapes from the structure of reasoning he brings to the text. This framework tells him, for example, what kinds of texts, what genres of discourse, with what different kinds of meaning, there can be.[9]

When a scholar is only seeking to establish which words form the text of Scripture, his latitude for alteration is very restricted. The questions concern only the grammatical form of single words or phrases, and whether a limited number of small questionable passages actually belong to the original manuscripts. Any changes to be made in the received text must be justified by reference to the manuscripts and the rules of grammar. This treatment of the text is the so-called lower criticism, and it can be said without qualification that there has not been a single determination by this lower criticism which has required any change in the traditional doctrine of the Christian Church.

Things stand differently with regard to what is called the higher criticism and it is with this higher or literary criticism that this chapter is concerned.[10] Although we are still dealing with judgements formed by the scholar's notions about what is reasonable and consistent, the critic has given himself much greater leeway. He undertakes, for example, to discriminate between what an historical figure is reported to have said or done according to the words of Scripture, and what he may be supposed really to have said or done. Much of the work of the higher criticism with the Gospels concerns such judgements. These are the discriminations by which scholarship has rejected as inauthentic most of the words ascribed to Jesus by the evangelists and determined that the miracles and the resurrection of Jesus are not historical events. The criteria are similarly subjective and give scope for radical dismemberment of the integrity of the scriptural books when the critic is endeavouring to distinguish the strata of a text. Here he is analysing a given text into layers, some of which he supposes were written earlier than others or by different people. For example, there is the so-called documentary hypothesis with respect to the first books of the Hebrew Scripture, J E P D. There is also the judgement of the date, sources, and temporal order of the gospel narratives – whether Mark is the earliest and was used by the others and whether the famous but undiscoverable Q existed.

Even questions about the date of books and their authorship involve philosophical and theological considerations. For among the determinations are judgements made by the scholar based on his own views about what is possible or appropriate, or as to whether such and such is the sort of thing that the historical figure in question is likely to have said or done, or whether this idea is consistent with that, or whether this idea or form is more primitive or more developed than that. For example, if the critic does not believe that miraculous prophecy is possible, he will date the prophecy after rather than before the events with which it deals. The ideas the critic brings to the text are thus crucial. If he is able to think in the way that those who wrote the text thought, he will be successful and make right judgements about it. On the other hand, if the scholar imports ideas far distant from the logic informing the text, the opposite will result. The intellectual assumptions of the scholar will be all-important.

Contemporary biblical critics are all aware of the importance for their enterprise of the intellectual framework brought to the text by the reader – the hermeneutic circle has become a preoccupation. But they differ about the effects of the assumptions on the argued conclusions of the scholar. None would agree with the great nineteenth-century critic Julius Wellhausen. His notion that 'philosophy does not precede but follows' biblical criticism would be thought too naive, as also his view that the philosophy of a critic can always be disentangled from his scholarly conclusions.[11] Here however the accord ends.

John Barton's recent *Reading the Old Testament: Method in Biblical Study* reveals the operation of the reader's intuition at every level of judgement about meaning. Moreover, Dr Barton shows the relation between the methods of biblical criticism and the history of literary criticism in the last century and a half. This extends our perception of the ways in which philosophical and theological presuppositions operate to influence literary judgements as he indicates how methods of literary criticism are related to philosophical and even political projects. For example, structuralism, a currently popular method, has Marxist associations as part of the destructive exposure of bourgeois forms of life, since structuralist interpretations expose the merely conventional character of meaning in literature.[12] On the other hand, Professor John Rogerson maintains that at least some conclusions of biblical scholarship are valid independently of their philosophical and theological presuppositions. He writes, 'Surely, the reconstruction of the history of Israel, or of the apostolic period, involves the use of an historical method unaffected by philosophy'.[13] His masterpiece, *Old Testament Criticism in the Nineteenth Century: England and Germany*, shows how the milieu was established first in Germany and then in England which made the reconstruction of the history of Israel, as the opposite of that indicated by the Old Testament itself, both thinkable and religiously acceptable. But Professor Rogerson wants to separate the motives of scholarship and the milieu, which allows its results to be accepted, from the results of this kind.[14] His position is unconvincing. In fact, he demonstrates the crucial role for the reconstruction of Israel's history as well as for the reception of it, of a new conception of religion 'as part of the universal experience of mankind', and of the Old Testament as 'part of the religious heritage of mankind'.[15] Reason then determines what are the logical stages of religion as universal phenomenon and reorders the history of Israel to conform to this pattern. It would seem wrong to dismiss for logical reasons the residual British empiricism of Professor Rogerson, but it may be fairly concluded that he has not proved his case.[16]

'NO DISCOVERY, ONLY HYPOTHESIS'

So, the degree to which the intellectual framework brought by the scholar to the study of Scripture is essential cannot be stressed too much. In some areas of biblical criticism it is the only determining element. Anthony Harvey, in his Bampton Lectures for 1980 published as *Jesus and the Constraints of History*, said forthrightly about the situation of the inquiry regarding the historical reliability of the Gospels:

> Nothing new has been discovered. The evidence is exactly the same as it always was – the bare text of the Gospels . . . There is no discovery, only an hypothesis.[17]

However, the philosophical and theological presuppositions determining the methods and conclusions of higher biblical criticism are questionably appropriate to the biblical text. Moreover, this was well known to those who began the higher criticism of Scripture. They intended a revolution which would separate Scripture from the pattern of interpretation which the tradition of the Church had given it. So when Professor C. S. Lewis, speaking as a literary critic, evaluated the work of biblical scholars, he said:

Whatever those men may be as biblical critics, I distrust them as critics. They seem to me to lack literary judgement, to be unperceptive about the very quality of the text they are reading.[18]

Despite the constant plea of biblical critics to allow them to treat these documents as any other books would be treated by modern scholarship, it seems that something else has been going on. To quote Lewis again: 'Everywhere except in theology there has been a vigorous growth of scepticism about scepticism.'[19]

Historians also find that the biblical scholarship of the contemporary time lacks scientific objectivity. The whole point of Anthony Harvey's *Jesus and the Constraints of History* is that if the standard of ordinary historical research were applied to the investigation of the gospel narratives, a great deal more could be affirmed as historical fact than critical biblical scholarship has conceded.

Indeed, when we turn to the founders of higher biblical criticism, we find that they were determined to separate themselves from the presuppositions of the text they were considering rather than the contrary. Thus David Friedrich Strauss, who in 1835 set moving the nineteenth-century critique of the New Testament with his *The Life of Jesus, Critically Examined*, wrote that an interpretation is 'impartial'

if it unequivocally acknowledges and openly avows that the matters narrated in these books must be viewed in a light altogether different from that in which they were viewed by the authors themselves.[20]

There is nothing more important to grasp than the point of this 'impartiality'. The aim of the criticism is to separate the Scripture from the Church and its doctrine, which claims to derive from Scripture and reciprocally to be that through which Scripture can be rendered intelligible. This reciprocity is necessary if both Scripture and Church are the work of the Holy Spirit. But, of course, the Church is already in the Scripture. Scripture is the religious literature of God's people, the old and the new Israel, and so the initial work of criticism is actually to rid itself of sympathy for the intellectual framework through which the Scriptures are constituted *as* Scripture, and through which they were constructed and interpreted. Making such an 'impartiality' as that of Strauss the necessary standpoint of criticism, would be the same as requiring that no Neoplatonist could write about Plato, or that no one could write about Homer unless he assumed Homer's gods to be self-conscious fictions. There is of course no possibility of writing without an interpretative framework. When Benjamin Jowett proposed in his piece for *Essays and Reviews*, 'On the Interpretation of Scripture', that we study Scripture as we do Plato and Sophocles without interpretative presuppositions, he showed only the magnitude of his naivety. For he himself wrote about Plato from the perspective of a nineteenth-century moral idealism which scholars now regard as inappropriate. Indeed, classical scholarship in this period was extraordinarily lacking in scientific objectivity. One finds the interpretative essays of the great Sophoclean scholar, Jebb, silly and it may be said that among the most difficult tasks of contemporary classical scholarship is that of overcoming the warped interpretative framework given the field by the nineteenth-century classical scholar and philosopher Friedrich Nietzsche.[21] An interpretative framework is necessary but there is no reason in principle why it ought not to be the traditional doctrine of the Church. None the less, the first enterprise of the higher criticism was to separate the Scripture from the doctrine of the Church in order to place it within a different philosophical and theological structure. What moved the higher criticism was not a change in the facts but rather a philosophical and theological change.

This feature of the biblical criticism of his time was well known to Dr Pusey, who wrote in his Preface to *Daniel the Prophet*, his great work in opposition to the first popularly known result of this scholarship in England, *Essays and Reviews* (1860):

> Disbelief of Daniel had become an axiom in the unbelieving critical school. Only, they mistook the result of unbelief for the victory of criticism. They overlooked the historical fact that the disbelief had been antecedent to the criticism. Disbelief had been the parent not the offspring of their criticism: their starting point, not the winning-post of their course.[22]

And it was equally clear to Dr Pusey's great biographer and disciple Henry Liddon, whose Bampton Lectures of 1866 are judged by Owen Chadwick to be the greatest of the nineteenth century.[23] They were entitled *The Divinity of Our Lord and Saviour Jesus Christ* and aimed to show that the Christ who had lost his divinity to scholarship had also lost that moral authority which the scholars wished to retain to use for their own purposes: 'If Christ is not God he is not good.' His notes on the various critical lives of Jesus exhibit his conviction that the conclusions of the critics are determined by their philosophical presuppositions and political purposes.[24]

We must attend in detail to these presuppositions. For unless we understand and overcome them we cannot hope to return to an interpretation of Scripture in harmony with the doctrine of the Church. In general, the new interpretative framework of the critical scholars originated in the nineteenth-century rebellion not only against the Christian doctrine as an intellectual system in which man could be at home as a spritual being; but also, this rebellion was a total revolt against the whole development of Western Culture and its defining idea that what is primary is a self-complete and all-determining intellectual and spiritual reality, a God who by his self-complete being of knowledge and love embraces the practical.

MARX, STRAUSS AND FEUERBACH

The most familiar and the most influential exposition of the contemporary (nineteenth- and twentieth-century) revolution is that of Karl Marx. Marx is explicit that his social and political revolution would not have been possible without the preceding theological revolution which provided its basis. Both involve a critique of Hegel who is regarded by theological and political radical alike as the last theologian of the traditional intellectual Christianity. At the end of 1843 and in the January of 1844, Marx began his *Contribution to the Critique of Hegel's Philosophy of Law* thus:

> For Germany the *criticism of religion* is in the main complete, and criticism of religion is the premise of all criticism. The *profane* existence of error is discredited after its *heavenly oratio pro aris et focis* has been disproved. Man, who looked for a superhuman being in the fantastic reality of heaven and found nothing there but the *reflection* of himself, will no longer be disposed to find but the *semblance* of himself, only an inhuman being, where he seeks and must seek his true reality. The basis of irreligious criticism is: *Man makes religion*, religion does not make man. Religion is the self-consciousness and self-esteem of man who

has either not yet found himself or has already lost himself again.[25]

D. F. Strauss had published his *Leben Jesu* in 1835. Ludwig Feuerbach, the critical theologian whose ideas figure directly and very prominently in the formation of Marx's thought, published his *Wesen des Christentums, The Essence of Christianity*, in 1841. After an initial letter to him in 1843, Marx sent Feuerbach a copy of his *Critique of Hegel's Philosophy of Law* on 11 August 1844 with a warm letter. His position on religion in the *Critique* is the same as that of the theologian Feuerbach, and Marx writes:

> . . . I am glad to have an opportunity of assuring you of the great respect and – if I may use the word – love, which I feel for you . . . You have provided . . . a philosophical basis for socialism and the Communists have immediately understood them in this way. The unity of man with man . . . the concept of the human species brought down from the heaven of abstraction to the real earth, what is this but the concept of society . . . The German artisans in Paris, i.e., the Communists amongst them, several hundreds, have been having lectures twice a week throughout this summer on your *Wesen des Christentums* . . .[26]

The Philosophical and Economic Manuscripts produced by Marx in 1844 contain much praise as well as criticism of Feuerbach as do also the *Theses on Feuerbach* of 1845. Feuerbach is again treated very seriously in *The German Ideology* written between November 1845 and August 1846 by Marx and Engels together.

For our purposes, the positions of Strauss, the biblical critic, Feuerbach, the critical theologian, and Marx are not philosophically and theologically different. Crucial to all three is a transformation of the idea of God and man by the bringing of heaven down to earth and by giving the attributes of divinity to the human race. Essential is the divinization of sensuous practical humanity. Marx goes beyond Strauss and Feuerbach only by working out the practical consequences more definitely. This is in virtue of his identification of alienation with private property, his class analysis of society, and his revolutionary programme based on this class analysis. Feuerbach remains too theoretical for Marx. Having made the sensuous world the primary reality – this makes his philosophy 'positive' – Feuerbach merely contemplates it:

Feuerbach's 'conception' of the sensuous world is confined on the one hand to mere contemplation of it and on the other hand to mere feeling.[27]

It is important to notice this difference between Marx and his theoretical predecessors Strauss and Feuerbach because the contemporary contextual theology to which we referred earlier is explicitly Marxist rather than Feuerbachian. That is, contextual theology is involved in providing prescriptions for revolutionary practice based on a class analysis of society; to this end it finds such class analysis in the teachings of Jesus. But we must deal with this later. What we must now grasp is the common position of the revolutionaries and that, as Pusey saw, the revolution took place first in theology.

THE NINETEENTH-CENTURY REVOLT

In 1828 Pusey wrote in his *Historical Enquiry into the probable causes of the rationalist character lately predominant in the Theology of Germany*:

The destructive and especially revolting characteristic of German rationalism consists of it having made its appearance within the Church, and in the guise of theology.[28]

The revolutionary philosophy and theology originating in the first half of the nineteenth century announced the end of the previous history of civilization in virtue of its discovery of the key by which the past was determined. Marx, for example, was able to say that 'communism is the riddle of history solved and knows itself to be this solution'.[29] What separates the old and new world is a new conception of man. The old Greek view of him as a rational animal had been further spiritualized by the Christian religion: 'The first man Adam was made a living soul; the last Adam was made a life-giving spirit' (1 Cor. 15.45).

By the time of Descartes the Christian notion that reality was spiritual through and through had reached such a point that Descartes was able to have confidence that men know the sensuous and natural world by knowing it through the knowledge of God.[30] It is against such an intellectual understanding of man and his world that the nineteenth-century post-Hegelian German philosophers and theologians rebelled. For them, man was alienated, lost to himself, by finding his truth in an intellectually conceived God and in a humanity represented as at home and reigning in the heavens, for example, in an ascended Jesus. Whereas in the past, spiritual progress was understood as the rise from sense to reasoning to union by knowledge and love with God; now the order was to be reversed. Human history was a movement from myth and its gods, to philosophy and its intellectual concepts to natural science and empirical knowledge of the physical world.

The notion that this is the movement of history is called positivism. In this progress man discovers himself positively, that is, he comes to be at home as a being in nature, his being as a physical, feeling, practical activity. The Marxist and existentialist forms of this new humanity are two sides of one coin. The two aspects are, on the one hand, man technologically mastering nature and, on the other, man seeking to return into unity with it. Both, however, presuppose that humanity has a being which is independent of the intellectual and spiritual substantiality, the Kingdom of God or of heaven. The Marxists will say that he is alienated or lost to himself when he attempts to find himself in such a reality; the existentialists (as in Heidegger) speak of humanity as what is thrown out of such a substantiality. In any case, for man to imagine his true home to be such an eternal intellectual heaven is false consciousness. Humanity projects an ideal of itself into heaven because it has not mastered this world or because it has lost unity with its physical and emotional self.

BEYOND THE ENLIGHTENMENT

To understand this nineteenth- and twentieth-century revolution, it is essential to distinguish it from the Enlightenment rebellion against Christianity and the substitution of reason for revelation, that is, a natural religion or deism, as the English called it. The founders of the nineteenth-century revolution thought of themselves as continuing enlightenment but, in at least two essential points, their enterprise was very different. First, as against the Enlightenment the true being of man was no longer centred in his rationality. While such a shift may be seen to have its origins in the Age of Reason (as in Rousseau and Hume), understanding the reconciliation with reality by reason to be negative as opposed to the true positive or practical and sensuous humanism is an altogether qualitative difference.[31] Secondly, this new revolution does not see the enlightenment it offers as freeing man from the superstition which is the Christian religion but rather as the true scientific insight into the authentic character of Christianity. The revolution soon became anti-Christian, as in Marx and Nietzsche, but the original leaders, for example Strauss and Feuerbach, understood themselves as a new kind of scientific theologian. Moreover, as we shall attempt to show below, while the revolutionary theology never gives up its presupposition of an independent, free, sensuous humanity, according to its own logic it develops a series of forms by which it identifies itself as the authentic discovery of the true historic and original Christianity. The revolutionary conception of Christianity is put thus by Feuerbach:

> The Incarnation is nothing else than the practical, material manifestation of the human nature of God . . . the need, the want of man – a want which still exists in the religious sentiment – was the cause of the Incarnation . . . the incarnate God is only the apparent manifestation of deified man; for the descent of God to man is necessarily preceded by the exaltation of man to God. Man was already in God, was already God himself, before God became man, i.e. showed himself as man . . . Hence in God I learn to estimate my own nature; I have value in the sight of God; the divine significance of my nature is become evident to me.[32]

Naturalistic humanism is true Christianity; this is the decisive belief of the nineteenth-century revolution. So it constitutes itself first of all by attacking the old intellectual doctrinal Christianity of the Church. The instrument of this demolition is an historical research which separates out as the truth the positive, empirically given, from the logical, the philosophical and doctrinal construct. Both a new dependence upon and a new understanding of history are essential parts of the revolutionary philosophical science or theology. Because man has turned away from the heaven of eternal essences or forms and refuses to find or establish the truth of his nature there, he must find himself and his God in history. Discerning the march of history becomes the only way of founding the substantial truth of ideas. So history becomes ideological at the same time that it becomes 'scientific'. It is too important to be left to the historians because it is necessary for determining what we can think and what we shall do. Conversely, the same confidence by which this naturalistic humanism feels itself to be the true Christianity enables it to subject the

Scriptures to this new historical scholarship so that therein may be discovered, as the original stratum of revelation, the new Christianity rather than the old.

What is found in the Bible as history changes in the shift from the Enlightenment to the nineteenth century just as the theological assumptions and methods change. When Henning Graf von Reventlow's *The Authority of the Bible and the Rise of the Modern World* is considered alongside John Rogerson's *Old Testament Criticism in the Nineteenth Century*, we have the appearance in English in a single year of a complete history of Old Testament criticism from its rise at the end of the Middle Ages to the end of the nineteenth century. Professor Rogerson summarizes the crucial differences between Enlightenment and post-Enlightenment results thus:

> By the close of the eighteenth century, no history of Israel had been written which presented the course of events in a fashion radically different from what is implied in the Old Testament. There had of course been attacks on the credibility of particular incidents as they were described in the Old Testament; but usually, ways could be found to salvage an historical core from the Old Testament presentation . . . Attack on individual miraculous or incredulous incidents did not lead, then, in late eighteenth-century German scholarship, to any desire to rewrite Old Testament history. The earliest chapters of Genesis were still held to contain authentic accounts of the experiences of earliest mankind, and the story of the Israelites taken as a whole could be seen as an educative process in which divine providence led the Israelites to the truths of religion prized above all in the Enlightenment: the unity of God and the immortality of the soul.[33]

In contrast, Julius Wellhausen's criticism, taken by Professor Rogerson as the synthetic result of nineteenth-century scholarship, reverses the history of Israelite religion from what the Old Testament itself implies. The revealed Law is not what is originative and constitutive of Israel; rather, the Law and its institutions are late. They are imposed by an abstract reason which confines the original individual freedom and spontaneity of the early and authentic Israel. Equally, New Testament historical scholarship separates the divine Hellenized Christ of faith from the true human Judaic Jesus of history.

Revolutionary theory thus gives itself the appearance of historical actuality. It is compelled to this as it has no other way to establish its truth, and it feels no compunction in reshaping history because the new humanism is confident that it is the true result of history.

NEW SPIRIT, OLD FORMS

Because the revolution is in one form or another a naturalized practical Christianity, it is capable of reinterpreting Christianity without any conscious antagonism towards the old forms. Indeed, the new spirit may be combined with a piety towards the past and at least the outer frame and aesthetic of the old Christianity. So we have confusion rather than an attack. An example of this is the neo-Thomism adopted by the Roman Church during the last hundred years. Beginning from practical political and apologetic assumptions of the contemporary world, and, in the spirit of that world, subordinating theology to practical ends as if it were an instrument of them, the Roman Church de-Platonized St Thomas Aquinas. That is, Thomas's philosophy was separated from his theology and God was understood existentially rather than as a self-thinking Platonic form, Being returned upon itself in thought.[34] A similar confusion has plagued the Tractarian and Anglo-Catholic return to tradition in so far as, opposing modern rationalism and the equation of Christian faith with a new scientific theology, it became itself anti-intellectual. Thus it tried to study the theology of the Fathers without thinking through their philosophical reasoning. Pusey himself located religion primarily in a practical and moral attitude and recommended a 'devout perusal' of the Fathers.[35] Equally problematic is the assumption by the successors of Pusey and Liddon who, following Charles Gore, believed

> not merely that credal orthodoxy and critical scholarship would prove to be ultimately reconcilable but also that properly understood they were reconciled already . . . therefore the question of priority between faith and reason was a purely hypothetical one.[36]

Such liberal catholicism was forced bit by bit to yield ground as the conflict between the 'assured results of modern criticism' and the credal formulations of the faith became manifest. Or again, we may find Anglo-Catholics at home with an existentialist theology like that

57

of Dr John Macquarrie which retains the most old-fashioned piety and traditional doctrines but has de-intellectualized them and refilled the centres with an opaque Heideggerian Being.[37]

Each of the forms of the revolutionary Christianity has produced or is producing a biblical scholarship which appears to give it historical actuality. The following examples are not intended to be a complete assemblage but should show the kinds of logic involved, indicate that the development has essentially reached its end, and manifest that we are confronted here with a factual account of the Scriptures only in a very special and historically relative sense.

KANTIAN POSITIVISM

The rationalism and its pietist reaction considered here remain within the Enlightenment as opposed to the succeeding revolutionary theology in so far as their tendency is towards a theoretical atheism rather than the divinized humanism of those who follow. None the less, they are essential to the development as they provide assumptions for their successors and pose the problem the revolutionary theology supposes that it solves.

The most important transitional figure between Enlightenment philosophy and contemporary revolutionary theology is Immanuel Kant.[38] Two notions of his are determinative of the direction of later thought, though how little he would have identified with their divinized natural humanism may be gathered from the title of his principal treatment of religion: *Religion within the Limits of Reason Alone*.[39] The first of his critical ideas is that reason is confined to ordering the world of sense appearances. Ultimately, this limits reason to natural science and provides the rationale of the otherwise incredible general assumption of critical biblical scholarship that the miraculous material in the Scriptures should be regarded as false except as it may be reinterpreted as the human conquest of nature. Even as late a writer as Rudolf Bultmann, who has an explicitly existentialist framework for interpreting Scripture, regards the miraculous as belonging to the mythical context of the New Testament which is unintelligible to modern man. The other notion of Kant which is determinative of what follows is that God is not known by pure, or theoretical, reason but rather is a postulate for man as a moral or practical being. In virtue of the philosophic developments subsequent to Kant, the revolutionary theology felt itself able to liberate man from subjection to such a God who dominates man as moral ideal but who never reveals himself to knowledge. God then becomes identical with progressive practical humanity. Nietzsche is instructive on the felt necessity and logic of this overturning of Kant.[40]

DE WETTE AND SCHLEIERMACHER

But before going on to the reaction against the Kantian God who remained an unattainable ideal, we must consider the biblical criticism which took as its unquestionable assumption the moral autonomy, the moral freedom, of Kant. This is the Old Testament work of W. M. L. de Wette and the life of Jesus by Friedrich Schleiermacher. It was de Wette who began to distinguish radically 'between the Old Testament story and what could be known about the actual facts'.[41] He was moved to this by what was to him the inadequacy between the true idea of Hebrew religion and the Judaism of the Old Testament. In his semi-autobiographical novel *Theodore, or the Doubter's Ordination* (1821), de Wette tells us what was decisive in determining his view of what true religion must be:

> Along with these biblical lectures, Theodore heard at the same time some lectures on morals from a Kantian philosopher, through which a completely new world was opened to him. The notions of the self-sufficiency of reason in its law giving, of the freedom of the will through which he was elevated above nature and fate, of the altruism of virtue which was its own justification and sought no reward, of pure obedience to the self-given moral law: all these notions gripped him powerfully, and filled him with a high self-awareness. Those shadowy ideas about the love of God and of Christ, about the new birth, about the rule of God's love in the human mind, all of which he still carried from the instruction of his schoolmaster, these he translated now into this new philosophical language, and so they appeared to him clearer and more certain.[42]

W. M. L. de Wette shows no hesitation in reconstructing and demythologizing the Bible in accord with the true philosophical idea of religion. Schleiermacher's position is much more ambiguous. Thus those who revolted against the limits of Enlightenment humanism learned from Schleiermacher, but heaped scorn on him for refusing to dissolve the divine into human freedom. This is the position of D. F. Strauss.[43] But Dr Pusey saw the other side of this inconsistency. In the midst of the rationalistic interpretation of Scripture which dominated German theology when Pusey visited in 1828, he found a pietist resistance, which though it conceded, in his view, too much to rationalism, none the less was leading theology in the right direction. That is, it refused to subordinate theology to philosophy and located religion in the affective and practical side of human personality. The leader of this movement was Schleiermacher:

> that great man, who, whatever be the errors of his system, has done more than any other (some very few perhaps excepted) for the restoration of religious belief in Germany.[44]

Schleiermacher granted to the positivistic rationalism sufficient that he excluded all other miracles save one, the unity of the universal and particular, God and man, in the historic individual Jesus Christ. It is instructive that, in such a theological perspective, the Gospel which was given a priority later assigned to Mark's, so that it provided the test of authenticity, measuring the others, was John's. Further, the miracle which is Christ, Schleiermacher interprets chiefly in moral categories. Christ is the pre-eminent embodiment of the ideal of truth and moral perfection which in virtue of its historical actuality in him draws humanity towards itself. God is thus present to man not as he is calculating, entangled in the relation of ends and means, but as he is actuated by a free moral spontaneity and feels therein an immediate relation to God. This understanding of Christ and of the nature of our union with him is the principle of Schleiermacher's *Life of Jesus*. His account not only demythologizes the scriptural miracles but requires a heterodox rejection of the existence of two wills in Christ – a human will and a divine will – as well as a treatment of Christ's nature which tends to docetism.

STRAUSS AND DIVINIZED HUMANITY

D. F. Strauss saw the instability in Schleiermacher's attempt to construct a Christian theology within the limits of Kant's development of enlightenment. As he indicates in the last part of his *Life of Jesus*, Strauss was convinced that the logical difficulties inherent in the unity of the universal and particular could not be resolved in an historical individual. The traditional theologies of the Church were all inadequate on this essential point as were the more recent attempts in Kant, Hegel, Schleiermacher and their followers. Only the human race itself was the adequate locus of divinity and he thought it to be the unity of spirit and nature; for him materialism and idealism should not be opposed.[45] The purpose of his *Life of Jesus* is to show that the universal and historical particular are not unified in the individual Jesus Christ and his enterprise is quite self-consciously philosophical. To F. C. Baur, he wrote in 1860 that for his procedure 'history is simply the means to a dogmatic, i.e. anti-dogmatic objective'.[46]

Miracle is the manifestation of the divine in the historical particular and so it must be presupposed false. But if the life of Jesus Christ is portrayed as miraculously fulfilling divine prophecy, then his life so understood must be regarded as the fictitious invention of the Church. By the miraculous operation of the Holy Spirit, the Church finds the unity of the Jesus of history and the Christ of her theological doctrine in Scripture. The presupposition of Strauss is that what vouchsafes this concordance is false: 'The presupposition on which the whole *Life of Jesus* was written was a denial of the miraculous and supernatural in the world.'[47] In other words, the starting-point of Strauss's history is the notion that spirit cannot operate except in the ordinary course of nature. This is not what his history discovers; it is the presupposition from which it begins, the assumption which both enables and requires the separation of the humanity and divinity united in Jesus Christ or, what is the same, the separation of the Jesus of history and the Christ of the Church's faith. No historical discovery necessitated that conclusion; the so-called history is rather a result of the presupposition. Strauss's *Life of Jesus* is intentionally destructive. His positive position, which is taken up by Feuerbach and Marx, is worth reproducing at length because it is the assumption of the whole revolutionary theology of the nineteenth and twentieth century in so far as it has a positive content:

> Is not the idea of the unity of the divine and human natures a real one in a far higher sense, when I regard the whole race of mankind as its realization, than when I single out one man as such a realization? Is not an incarnation of God from eternity, a truer one than an incarnation limited to a particular point of time?

61

This is the key to the whole of Christology, that, as subject of the predicate which the Church assigns to Christ, we place, instead of an individual, an idea; but an idea which has an existence in reality, not in the mind only, like that of Kant. In an individual, a God-man, the properties and functions which the Church ascribes to Christ contradict themselves; in the idea of the race, they perfectly agree. Humanity is the union of the two natures – God become man, the infinite manifesting itself in the finite, and the finite spirit remembering its infinitude; it is the child of the visible Mother and the invisible Father, Nature and Spirit; it is the worker of miracles, in so far as in the course of human history the spirit more and more completely subjugates nature, both within and around man, until it lies before him as the inert matter on which he exercises his active power; it is the sinless existence, for the course of its development is a blameless one, pollution cleaves to the individual only, and does not touch the race of its history. It is Humanity that dies, rises, and ascends to heaven, for from the negation of its phenomenal life there ever proceeds a higher spiritual life; from the suppression of its mortality as a personal, national, and terrestrial spirit, arises its union with the infinite spirit of the heavens. By faith in this Christ, especially in his death and resurrection, man is justified before God: that is, by the kindling within him of the idea of Humanity, the individual *man* participates in the divinely human life of the species.[48]

MORAL IDEALISM

Some, like Feuerbach and Marx, carried further the humanism of Strauss in a direction incompatible with the existence of religion but there was also a more conservative reaction by which a liberated humanity might deal with the Gospels in a less negative manner than Strauss had done. F. C. Baur, the great leader of the so-called Tübingen School, had taught D. F. Strauss, but his relations with him were difficult. Baur was prepared to defend him from the attacks of the orthodox, but he found his *Life of Jesus* too negative from the perspective of 'a true and real history'[49] and the two were not able to remain friends. The Tübingen School provided the stimulus for a great flowering of historical and literary biblical scholarship in the second half of the nineteenth century. Much of it, like that of Lightfoot, Westcott and Hort at Cambridge or that of Charles Gore's liberal Catholics with their centre in Oxford, was conservative at least in the sense that it assumed that the new scholarship and traditional Christianity of the creeds were compatible, or better, that the first would illumine the second.[50] The compromise between catholicism and criticism attempted by Gore evoked scepticism and sorrow in H. P. Liddon, the disciple and biographer of Dr Pusey, who had held one of the new chairs in biblical interpretation created during the university reform. For Charles Gore was the first Principal of Pusey House, and so *Lux Mundi* appeared from the memorial to the Tractarians which Liddon had hoped would carry on their anti-modernist work. But what underlay this confidence in a synthesis between modern historical scholarship and Christianity? There is philosophically a certain return to Kant which is evident in the location of the religious impulse in man in his practical and affective aspects, in an emphasis on the 'regulative' rather than speculative character of Christian doctrine, and in the moral progressivism of Albrecht Ritschl. This is represented in England by the book which made the new biblical scholarship popularly known, *Essays and Reviews* (1860).

The aspects of this stage in the modern treatment of the Bible are displayed in the essays of the work. Baden-Powell wrote 'On the Study of the Evidences of Christianity' in a rationalistic vein which took the positivism of the natural science of the time as unquestionable. Benjamin Jowett, who as Master was largely responsible for the recent prestige of Balliol College, Oxford, where he trained the administrators of the British Empire, contributed an essay 'On the Interpretation of Scripture'. This piece contains his plea for an unbiased historical reading of Scripture, undisturbed by philosophical and theological prejudices and considerations, which prevent its sense from being clear in the way that the meaning of Sophocles or Plato is. Criticism and a personal religion are not incompatible, indeed the fight against theological prejudice and against the passions of the individual soul are but two fronts of the one battle. So the progress of science and of historical criticism against prejudice and passion are Christianized in Powell and Jowett. But Frederick Temple in his 'Education of the World', which led off the volume, expressed most naively and directly what enabled the later nineteenth century both to identify modern science and the true historical sense of Christian religion and also to equate the imperial interests of European states, as the vehicles of this modern Christian religion, with the good of mankind as a whole.

Dr Temple compares the growth and moral progress of an individual with that of the whole human race and concludes:

> . . . The successive generations of men are days in this man's life. The discoveries and inventions which characterize the different epochs of the world's history are his works. The creeds and doctrines, the opinions and principles of the successive ages, are his thoughts. The state of society at different times are his manners. He grows in knowledge, in self-control, in visible size, just as we do. And his education is in the same way and for the same reason precisely similar to ours.[51]

> This education and progress of humanity has consequences for religion: Physical science, researches into history, a more thorough knowledge of the world they inhabit, have enlarged our philosophy beyond the limits which bounded that of the Church of the Fathers. We can acknowledge the great value of the forms in which the first ages of the Church defined the truth, and yet refuse to be bound by them; we can use them, and yet endeavour to go beyond them . . . In learning this new lesson, Christendom needed a firm spot on which she might stand, and has found it in the Bible . . . the Bible, from its very form, is exactly adapted to our present want. It is a history; even the doctrinal parts of it are cast in a historical form, and are best studied by considering them as records of the time at which they were written, and as conveying to us the highest and greatest religious life of that time. Hence we use the Bible . . . not to override, but to evoke the voice of conscience. When conscience and the Bible appear to differ, the pious Christian immediately concludes that he has not really understood the Bible. Hence, too, while the interpretation of the Bible varies slightly from age to age, it varies always in one direction.[52]

THE 'ACQUISITION OF TOLERATION'

The tendency is the growth of toleration. When the Bible is placed within the history of a moral progress of mankind understood as the 'acquisition of that toleration which is the chief philosophical and religious lesson of modern days',[53] then it evokes the voice of conscience and arouses it to confidence in its private judgements. Because the Bible and the history of its interpretation belong to the stages of the education of mankind, we must not be afraid to investigate them from the perspective of the modern natural, philosophic and historical sciences:

> . . . every day makes it more and more evident that the thorough study of the Bible, the investigation of what it teaches and what it does not teach, the determination of the limits of what we mean by its inspiration, the determination of the degree of authority to be ascribed to the different books, if any degrees are to be admitted, must take the lead of all other studies. He is guilty of high treason against the faith who fears the result of any investigation, whether philosophical, or scientific, or historical.[54]

There are evidently many unresolved problems in this optimistic reconciliation of modern science, historical method, and philosophy. It is hard to see how the merely historical knowledge of the Scriptures can be of any religious use to a humanity which, it is supposed, has progressed spiritually beyond them, unless moral progress and toleration be taken as their actual historical teaching. This is what was found, and the true Jesus was portrayed as a moral teacher, a Jewish Socrates. The divinity of Christ and the desire for mystic union with the divine power present in the death and resurrection of the God-man was discovered to be Pauline corruption and Hellenic overlay. In any case, both the belief in the moral progress of mankind and faith in the unambiguous benefit of the development of science are casualties of the twentieth century. Progressive humanism and science are too closely associated with the overwhelming suffering and destruction of mankind and nature in this century. But before it became plain to everyone that moral progress, the growth of toleration, the education of the world and the European empires were not the Christian and human hope, Friedrich Nietzsche destroyed their philosophical basis, Karl Barth the theological ground, and Albert Schweitzer the New Testament scholarship on which they rested.

Nietzsche despised the bourgeois culture which supposed that it could leave behind the metaphysical content of Christianity and translate what remained into its own morality and religion of science.

Karl Barth was moved to his reaction against the liberal rationalist theology of the nineteenth century by its humiliation with Germany in the Great War; the identification of liberal theology with the progress of civilization had prevented the Church distinguishing its aims from those of Kaiser Wilhelm. Albert Schweitzer showed that, owing to this identification, the liberal scholars had been unable to hear the meaning of Christ's preaching of the coming Kingdom of God:

> . . . one need only read the Lives of Jesus written since the sixties, and notice what they have made of the great imperious sayings of the Lord, how they have weakened down His imperative world-contemning demands upon individuals, that He might not come into conflict with our ethical ideals, and might tune His denial of the world to our acceptance of it . . . We have made Jesus hold another language with our time from that which He really held . . . It is nothing less than a misfortune for modern theology that it mixes history with everything and ends by being proud of the skill with which it finds its own thoughts – even to its beggarly pseudo-metaphysic with which it has banished genuine speculative metaphysic from the sphere of religion – in Jesus and represents Him as expressing them.[55]

Schweitzer, by disclosing Jesus to be the Son of Man come to preach the end of the world in the coming of God's Kingdom, separated Jesus and his historical world from the bourgeois satisfaction with the moral progress of their world and indicated the general character of the next stage of our history. But before we look at the New Testament scholarship of existentialism, we need to attend to what it made of the Old Testament.

D. F. Strauss and his liberal successors brought out the self-creative side of modern divinized humanism; theirs was a theology expressing the more Marxist and technological aspect of the connected poles of revolutionary culture. Thus, for Strauss the biblical miracles were myths about the power of mankind to subdue nature, and for the moral idealists the coming of the Kingdom Christ proclaimed was the moral progress of humanity embodied in the triumph of modern natural and historical science. But there is another side to the divinization of man as sensuous and practical. If a spiritual heaven is the self-projection of an alienated humanity, then it must be hidden or disappear for authentic man so that he may be at home not in the *conquest* of nature, but rather by returning *within* it. The revolt against technology, which simultaneously presupposes what it loathes, is existentialism. Friedrich Nietzsche and Martin Heidegger are the greatest philosophical theologians of this stage of revolutionary thought. Its first major biblical scholar is Julius Wellhausen.

EXISTENTIALISM: JULIUS WELLHAUSEN

Professor Wellhausen's name is associated with the so-called documentary hypothesis regarding the structure of the Old Testament. Scholars claim to be able to distinguish under the text as we have it strata distinguishable from one another by the language and interests of their authors. These various sources were then woven together by editors, themselves belonging to one or the other of these source traditions which are customarily designated by letters, J E D P. So, for example, it is maintained that there are two accounts of the creation of man in Genesis: one belongs to the Priestly source, P (1.1–2.4a), the other to the source which called God Jahveh, J (2.4b–4.25).[56] In fact, Julius Wellhausen did not invent this hypothesis; it was developed over a considerable time by scholars and by itself did not arouse fervent opposition.[57] But, Julius Wellhausen's work was synthetic and his union of the hypothesis with other elements of the intellectual world of German biblical criticism did away with this openness. For Professor Wellhausen employed the hypothesis as part of the rediscovery of the true religion of Israel as opposed to the Judaism of the Old Testament itself. This was the conclusion of the work of de Wette and Wilhelm Vatke.[58] Thus, the Old Testament becomes a source book for the history of religion rather than Scripture.[59] Further, in accord with his conceptions, which approximate philosophically to the existentialism of Nietzsche, he determined the order of the developmental stages of Jewish religion to be such that the Mosaic Law appears not as the origin of the nation's religious life but as a decadent decline. This is nicely summarized by John Rogerson thus:

> The study of Israelite religion was strongly influenced by philosophical theories about the nature of religion that were current in Germany between 1800 and 1850. Of particular importance was a view that distinguished between the spontaneous religion of a people in its 'infancy' and a cultic, priestly, doctrinal form of religion into which the spontaneous form developed. In

67

the 1870's, Julius Wellhausen . . . presented a version of the history of Israelite religion which distinguished three phases, each phase corresponding to a document or documents which made up the Pentateuch. The documents J and E . . . were evidence of a spontaneous early phase in Israel's religion, before the onset of the second phase in which there was concern for the centralization of worship and cultic regulation, as reflected in the D document . . . After the Exile, Israelite religion was completely dominated by the priests and by the minutiae of cultic regulation as seen in the Priestly document . . . Much of the material traditionally ascribed to Moses, for example, the institution of the priesthood and the sacrificial system, was, according to this approach, no earlier than the sixth century BC. Critical scholarship . . . had produced a description of the history of Israelite religion radically at variance with that in the Old Testament itself.[60]

But there was no necessity for this reversal except what derived from the extremely doubtful existentialist prejudices of Wellhausen about what is original and authentic in religion and what is late and decayed. Nietzsche, reacting against the abstract intellectuality and restrictive social life of the modern technological state, wished to return to a free spontaneous human being at home in his senses and impulses; he wanted without really thinking it possible to return to an animal existence within nature. So Nietzsche idealized the Homeric heroes whom he portrayed in this way.[61] Wellhausen simply does the same for the early Israelites, but his objective evidence can at most show that the Priestly written documents are *edited* late. It does not demonstrate that their content, which transmitted orally or in fragments from Moses might well have formed Israel as a nation, did not belong to the origins of Mosaic religion. Professor Wellhausen is forthright about his biases:

. . . the history of the ancient Israelites shows us nothing so distinctly as the uncommon freshness and naturalness of their impulses. The persons who appear always act from the constraining impulse of their nature, the men of God not less than the murderers and adulterers: they are such figures as could only grow up in the open air. Judaism, which realized the Mosaic constitution and carried it out logically, left no free scope for the individual; but in ancient Israel the divine right did not attach to the institution but was in the Creator Spirit, in individuals. Not only did they speak like the prophets, they also acted like judges and kings, from their own free impulse, not in accord with an outward norm, and yet, or just because of this, in the spirit of Jehovah.[62]

This anti-intellectual and anti-institutional bias characterizes the whole of the existentialist phase of the revolutionary theology.

EXISTENTIALISM: RUDOLF BULTMANN

Julius Wellhausen represents in biblical scholarship the Nietzschean form of the existentialist stage of revolutionary theology in which the flight from modern reason and institutions attempts to find satisfaction in a natural spontaneous individual freedom.[63] Rudolf Bultmann derives his principles from a twentieth-century existentialist philosopher. Bultmann continues and modifies the demythologizing of the New Testament begun by D. F. Strauss so as to make the Scripture speak to contemporary humanity as its character is analysed by Heidegger.[64] For man seeking to return within Being in its separation from thought (Heidegger's view of our situation) the true Christian religion is the proclamation of a Kingdom of Heaven which must be contradicted by everything objectively known:

> There is no difference between security based on good works and security built on objectifying knowledge. The man who desires to believe in God must know that he has nothing at his own disposal on which to build his faith, that he is, so to speak, in a vacuum.[65]

True faith looks for no evidence of the Kingdom now, it belongs only to the future:

> this hope or this faith may be called readiness for the unknown future that God will give. In brief, it means to be open to God's future in the face of death and darkness.[66]

This requires the demythologizing of Scripture in the sense that all evidence of the supernatural as objective must be eliminated.

69

Bultmann interprets out the miracles as did Strauss, but Bultmann does so on the ground that they belong to mythology:

> which speaks about this [divine] power inadequately and insufficiently because it speaks about it as if it were a worldly power ... Myths give worldly objectivity to that which is unworldly.[67]

The resurrection is the chiefest of these miracles and is completely mythological.[68] We must place our faith in these myths but we must on no account be able in any way to know the supernatural, invisible, divine world as present and real. According to the principle that faith to be faith must contradict everything known historically or philosophically to be true, the Scriptures are criticized and the authentic Jesus is distinguished from the ever faithless Church which always seeks to have reason for what it believes.[69]

This same Heideggerian existentialism can be used to interpret the Old Testament as well. Anthony Phillips has written on Genesis 1–11 in *Lower than the Angels*. The whole work is in the title. Man is lower than the angels. He must not aspire here to their intellectual existence. He must live in and struggle with the darkness of this world without the knowledge of the light of the realms above. Adam's sin is his aspiration for such angelic knowledge and Dr Phillips says of Jesus, the new Adam, that he died a believer without knowledge. Authentic man

> cannot penetrate what lies behind creation – the divine realm, heaven itself (Genesis 11). In the relationship between God and man, God remains God and man man . . . This is why Christians regard Jesus as the perfect *adam*, for he alone of all men fully grasped his full human potential in his perfect relationship with his Father in which he did not grasp at divinity (Philippians 2.6), but was content to die as man, an agnostic believer.[70]

Dr Phillips thus presupposes the correctness of Bultmann's interpretation of the statements of Jesus about his knowledge of the Father ascribed to him by John's Gospel; Bultmann maintains they are the interpolations of heretical gnostic mythologizers.

BIBLICAL THEOLOGY

Far more important in the history of the interpretation of the Old

Testament in the twentieth century is the work of the biblical scholars who operated within the assumptions of the so-called biblical theology. They attempted to find the structure, logic and language of theology directly in the Scriptures. Traditionally philosophy had provided the medium by which biblical revelation in its various genres – history, poetry, law, prophecy – was recast by the Church into its doctrine and theology. During the patristic period when the creeds were formed, as well as later, the medium was that of Greek philosophy. From its origins, the revolutionary theology strove with all its might to de-Hellenize the Christian religion. At first this was in order to separate it from the Church and its intellectual system. Now, with biblical theology, the aim is to find the theology of the Church directly and immediately in God's revelation in the Scripture. Christian man is still, none the less, to be prevented from ascending out of a total and serious practical struggle in this world into heavenly contemplation or mystical union with God. It is essential, therefore, to the work of biblical theology that it set up a complete opposition between Greek and philosophical patterns of thought and practice on the one hand, and biblical, Hebrew or Semitic patterns, on the other. The latter are to be normative for Christianity. Professor James Barr summarizes the opposition nicely:

> the contrast may be expressed as the contrast between the divisive, distinction-forming, analytic type of Greek thought and the totality type of Hebrew thought. Hence, . . . Greek thought is supposed to have been productive of splits and distinctions unknown to the Hebrews – being and becoming, reality and appearance, time and eternity, body and soul, spirit and matter, group and individual.[71]

Happily, the whole enterprise is now exploded, because, on less biased examination, the required structures could not be found in Hebrew or Semitic linguistic forms, and because it occurred to thinkers that biblical theology mistook the distance and difference there must be between the Bible and theology – both lost their real shape and character when they were confused.[72] Unfortunately, until these results become generally known we endure sermons maintaining that Christians must believe that action is all, and that Christianity and covenant, soul and body, etc., are the same, but this too will pass. What gives the biblical theology its power of endurance is its coherence with the thought of the greatest theologian of this century, Karl Barth.[73]

KARL BARTH

Karl Barth's theology is existentialist in the Heideggerian sense described previously. Philosophy neither enables the Christian to rise towards heavenly knowledge nor does it mediate between the Word of God and the hearer in order to explain how the latter can understand what is addressed to him. Barth, like Heidegger, is opposed to all onto-theo-logy, the mixing of the Greek and the Hebrew.[74] In addition, the relation of this late stage of the revolutionary theology to its nineteenth-century origins shows itself in Barth's appreciation of Feuerbach. Feuerbach is for Barth wrong about God, but his anthropology is an advance:

> Feuerbach has . . . a head start over modern theology . . . I speak of his resolute antispiritualism . . . or positively, of his anthropological realism . . . He is concerned with the whole reality (heart and stomach) of man. It is only when one is thus concerned that one can in truth speak of God.[75]

A little later in the same work Barth claims that Christian theology has failed to see the real Old and New Testament which speaks in this down-to-earth way and consequently

> the suspicion has been aroused that in its most highly human idealism, Christian theology's 'God', or its otherworldliness, may be human illusion in the face of which it is well to remain true to the earth.[76]

Or, put more directly, Barth regards modern materialism as a justified reaction to the spiritual and intellectual representation of man and God by the old theology. He is equally harsh in his criticism of mysticism, the experience of union with God. And so the existentialist phase of the revolutionary theology retains the anthropology with which the revolt originated, but now there is also a God who speaks to man from an absolute divine transcendence. It is, however, impossible in principle and incomprehensible in fact that man should hear God.

CONTEXTUAL OR MARXIST THEOLOGY

We come now to the end of the development of the revolutionary theology of the last 150 years and its result seems to be that theology finally arrives at the position of Karl Marx. For the theology of hope or liberation, praxis, or contextual theology criticizes existential theology as too subjectivist, and the position of Strauss and Feuerbach as too idealist.[77] Moving beyond these earlier stages of the revolution, it finds the Christian hope in an historical resurrection of Christ from the dead, yet this resurrection is an event not in the past or the present but in the future, a future which only occurs in the political transformation of the world. This final and decisive move into practical political history as against all forms of personal or intellectual transcendence is achieved only when theology finally comes to terms with Marx, and this theology explicitly calls itself Marxist.[78] The pre-eminent praxis theologian, Jurgen Moltmann says:

> . . . an integration of Catholics, Protestants, Liberals, and Marxists is possible once all of them learn to look beyond their own systems forward to the future of the realm of freedom.[79]

Christ, as he is experienced in the misery and oppression of the present reality, is not the resurrected but the crucified Christ:

> The Christian resurrection faith is thus historically unverifiable . . . [it] is not verifiable 'as yet'.[80]

Only at the end of history (Marx also saw the revolution as the end of history) will the resurrection of Christ be known. But this does not mean that historical research is useless; its function

> lies . . . not so much in the effort somewhere to position ourselves in the process of history on the safe foundation of fixed facts, but on the contrary, in the permanent criticism which dissolves all facts in open processes and therefore all certainties and all ties in expectations and liberties.[81]

This dissolution is necessary because the Kingdom in which Christ's resurrection will be known is one in which all the structures of the political and social power have been dissolved.

There is in Moltmann the existentialist desire to overcome modern technology:

73

> In view of what is meant and what is promised when we speak of the raising of Christ, it is therefore necessary to expose the profound irrationality of the rational cosmos of the modern, technico-scientific world.[82]

But the openness of the new society – or, put another way, the revolutionary destruction of all previous order – is total. For Moltmann, the traditional understanding of the doctrine of the Trinity, which he calls 'monarchism', must be overcome and all that belongs to it:

> The notion of a divine monarchy in heaven and on earth . . . generally provides the justification for earthly domination – religious, moral, patriarchal or political domination – and makes it a hierarchy, a 'holy rule' . . . The doctrine of the Trinity which evolves out of the surmounting of monotheism for Christ's sake, must therefore also overcome this monarchism, which legitimates dependency, helplessness, and servitude . . . The doctrine of the Trinity . . . developed as a doctrine of freedom must for its part point towards a community of men and women without supremacy and without subjection.[83]

Yet the work of theology is not theorizing; theology is political action itself:

> Concrete attention must be paid to religious problems of politics and to laws compulsions and the vicious circles which for economic and social reasons constrict, oppress or make impossible the life of man and living humanity. The freedom of faith is lived out in political freedom. The freedom of faith therefore urges men on towards liberating actions.[84]

THE 'FUTURE REALM OF FREEDOM'

This theology of a 'future realm of freedom' seems to have lost all actual contemplative and theoretical freedom in the present, but for its adherents it seems the true realization of everything accomplished in the earlier stages of the revolution. It demythologizes the 'false heaven' of religion by means of an historically progressive humanism which seriously confronts the problem of oppressive institutions. Like existentialist theology, it is agnostic and critical of everything supposed to be objectively present. It does not idolize the current structures of civilization, neither the remnants of the old state or the patriarchial family nor the scientific bureaucracies by which modern men and nature are engineered and exploited, but opens us to a transcendent future. By making theology into praxis, it realizes and makes historically actual the revolutionary hope; that is, it turns theology into the very process of political and social, psychological and personal liberation. To do this, it need only add one tool to those already in the hands of biblical scholars. Scholars need to use their knowledge of the context of the various elements of Scripture in order to understand the structures of oppression and the Christian solution for them.

Obviously this may take many forms, including the discernment of the 'oppressively sexist' structures of life and language. It will be necessary to understand how Scripture was written and interpreted from the perspective of 'man-as-wielder-of-power'. One of the requirements of contextual 'advocacy scholarship' will thus be the 'feminist hermeneutic of suspicion'.[85]

The example I have chosen shows the use of contextual theology to discover that Jesus, like Marx, understood the class structures of his time and not only did he set his proclamation of God's Kingdom against them but also he pointed the way to overcome them. In his 'Address for Ken Hamilton's Retirement' for the Atlantic School of Theology, Dogmatics Professor Martin Rumscheidt offered the following 'materialistic' analysis of the Parable of the Labourers in the Vineyard (Matthew 20.1–16). Such an analysis is necessary because 'the concern with individual life and practice is directly proportional . . . to the kind of church and theology observable in the Western world now: namely the community of those who lord it over others at home and elsewhere'.

> The aim of the materialist consideration of Scripture is practical: Materialistic reading of a text or whole document wants to know out of what socio-political milieu or milieus a text came originally, how those socio-political milieus of the process of tradition and canonization shaped the text, to whom the text was addressed and who now repeats it. But the reading also wants to illumine our own existing socio-political milieus with texts that

75

the all renewing, humanizing practice of messianic discipleship can advance in the historical process of humanizing human existence of making and keeping human life human.

Dr Rumscheidt uses Luise Schottroff's 'materialistic reading' of Matthew 20.1-16:

> . . . one must not abstract what is said of God and of people from the fact that the parable puts those matters into the context of the labour market . . . The parable does not concern itself with pay for work done or fairness in return for services rendered: it addresses the stance of those who because of what they describe as their performance claim privilege over others . . . The context of the parable is privilege, the belief that, being equal, some of us are nevertheless to have greater privilege, greater power.

We can move from such an analysis to action in our current world; it is to move towards 'the reality of solidarity'.

> And that is exactly the iconoclastic and constructive service historical materialism makes towards Christian theology, exegesis preaching and institutionalizing. It undermines the false refuge to the so-called eternal verities which truly are no more than opiate dished out to those whom one dominates while pretending to believe that we are all created equal . . . the parable has a precise, political aim: the transformation of the society which has come to stratify itself along the hard and fast lines of privilege, of life-style, of material possession and power . . . The gospel leads on to knowledge, but not knowledge as the perception of things as they are but as a consciously employed instrument in the transformation of the human community . . .

My discovery of the biblical scholarship of contextual theology is one of the occasional causes of this essay; this, for two reasons. First, because the philosophical and theological absurdity of a Marxist Christianity is matched by the obviously arbitrary subjectivity of the biblical 'scholarship'. In realizing the revolutionary theology by equating theology with praxis, the movement has not only come full circle but also has exposed that it is not theology at all. Theology as praxis claims to have faith and hope in a God who has no existence except in the political-social-personal revolutionary striving of his people. Trust in an infinite divine power which can transform the miserable actuality of existence is the only possible ground of the endless restless human work to criticise and overturn every power. Socialist anarchy, or the solidarity of perfectly liberated natural individuals, is a contradiction incapable of any stable realization. God, infinite, omnipotent, perfectly self-complete and so able to accomplish his will through the whole course of human and natural finitude is the assumption of this theology, and yet is altogether denied by it.[86] The logical impossibility of the theology is mirrored in the end of all pretence of objectivity in its biblical 'scholarship'. To make the sexual-personal or political-economic context of the Bible the chief focus of our reading of it is self-evidently arbitrary, anachronistic and self-interested.

Contemporary liberation theology uses criticism while remaining completely sceptical about the possibility of any objectivity in scholarship. It does not wish to become conscious of presuppositions so as to strive towards a theological objectivity. Rather, it is necessary to its position that there be no historical resurrection, so that one can be made (see Moltmann at note 80 above). Structuralism is Marxist because it aims to expose all systems of meaning as conventional, bourgeois, so as to facilitate the revolution (see note 12 above). The feminists oppose any objectivity as just another form of male domination, again using reason to undermine the revelation of God in feminine sensuality and in fidelity to the life of feelings and emotions. A theology or methodology of the Word is but another trick of 'man-as-wielder-of-power' to persuade women from their interests and perspectives. Unfortunately, the scepticism into which biblical scholarship has fallen plays into the hands of this 'liberation'. When biblical scholars conclude 'if there is one tendency of biblical criticism it has been my aim to call in question, it is this tendency to seek the normative',[87] they are helpless against the contemporary forces of sceptical but determined revolution.

ACTIVITY AS A SIGN OF LIFE

The second reason Marxist theology arouses concern is that it is more directly practical than the earlier forms of the revolutionary theology and threatens the Church and the world more immediately. The Church has idolized the practical for so long it no longer has the power to resist even this absurdly contradictory 'theology'. Examples abound; one of the complaints of my New Testament professors at seminary was that critical biblical scholarship never got out of the study; one could rarely persuade the clergy to teach it to people. It was unappealing to clergy once out of theological college because it so opposed the doctrinal, liturgical, and devotional use of the New Testament which was primarily how people expected to employ Scripture. Indeed in the diocese of Nova Scotia, M. F. Toal's *The Sunday Sermons of the Great Fathers* is more used by the clergy under forty than any critical commentary.[88] Those clergy who did try providing their people with the results of biblical criticism usually did not last long in the parish. But this new materialist reading of the Scriptures could have a different fate. Its concrete practicality makes it attractive to those who think activity in the Church is the sign of life. If the Church discovers a vocation as a socio-economic, political and personal liberation movement, then the new 'scholarship' could come out of the study into the streets.[89]

This change in the role and character of theology has consequences for the study of theology. Seminaries are reorganizing their curricula to accord with the requirements of method in contextual theology. Theology is now to be done. It is to become praxis and biblical study will become an ideological activity, i.e. a means for reflecting on the world for the sake of its transformation:

> The gospel leads on to knowledge . . . as a consciously employed instrument in the transformation of the human community into a community where the honoured title *human* is neither a mere rhetorical phrase nor an utopian figment.[90]

This will certainly remove biblical scholars from the study into the streets, a removal just as threatening to them as to the Church and the world.

There is, however, an ironic other side to this half-realized marriage of Liberation Theology and biblical criticism which awakens hope. The last stage of the revolutionary theology is too late. Just because it can so explicitly use biblical criticism to turn Scripture into a constantly revised ideological tool, ideas of use for the multi-varied forms of liberation, it depends upon an awareness which has also overtaken biblical scholars generally that the methods of higher biblical criticism do not produce objective results. Biblical scholars are becoming aware of the philosophical, subjective, and ideological factors in the history of critical scholarship. There is a preoccupation with the problem of hermeneutics, the categories of interpretation, and with the question of method in theology. The end of biblical theology and a recognition of the difference between the forms of Scripture and of theology has a result like scepticism. John Barton's conclusion is not merely his own. Others recognize with him that the normative question, the question as to how we should read the Bible 'can never be shown by biblical criticism of any kind, but only by theological argument lying outside the biblical critic's province'.[91] The urgent search is for a restoration of a fruitful relation between theology and biblical study.

RETURNING TO A THEOLOGICAL UNDERSTANDING

How does the scholar bring a theological framework to the study of Scripture without arbitrariness and self-serving interest? Biblical scholars like John Rogerson, Ernest Nicholson, James Barr, Brevard Childs, John Barton, von Reventlow, reflecting on the history of modern biblical study, find this deeply troubling for the possibility of proceeding according to the already established lines of thought and methods of approach.[92] The history of critical scholarship can be written because it is in some way complete; awareness of the history now places the scholar outside the presuppositions of his science. What formerly appeared as objective scientific fact now seems to have been determined by the philosophical and doctrinal assumptions of the scholars.

The result is that the revolutionary theology must stand on its own without the support of historical critical science. This accords with its own principles as well as with the actual position of biblical studies. Moltmann's historical critical study can only destroy and dissolve, the existent facts establish nothing, only the future can verify history. So the only basis of the revolutionary theology is the determination to remake the world by divinizing the practicality of natural man, by fully liberating him as a social animal. But this is in fact the assumption from which the whole movement began, so we now return to it naked and exposed for what it is. This is the 'late humanism' of which von Reventlow traces the history and shows to be the tail-end of the heterodoxies of the modern Western tradition: the spiritualizing dualism and rationalizing moralism which make incomprehensible grace mediated through history. The heterodox tendency destroys grace and history alike. He also writes so that he 'can clarify existing intrinsic presuppositions and help us to overcome them by making us aware of them'.[93]

BACK TO DR PUSEY

We return, then, to the origins of the contemporary treatment of the Bible in the first third of the nineteenth century. But this time our attention is focused on the reaction against the revolution. In so far as our problem is to restore the relation between theology and biblical scholarship, between the ecclesiastical tradition and the Scripture,[94] we must now attend to those who turned to the Church and its traditional forms and patterns of thought in the revolutionary situation. They have been with us as opponents to the history we have traced, until finally they were drawn into it. The reaction back into older forms of doctrine and devotion took many shapes in the nineteenth century and we have not even noted the Protestant and evangelical enterprises. The resistance in the Roman Church, which was initially organized and propelled against the foe with great energy as a consequence of the first Vatican Countil, did not give way until its startling and complete collapse with the second Vatican Council.[95] Just when the Roman Church took over the warfare, the Tractarian reaction surrendered to the new biblical criticism. As we have indicated, the eventual conquest of the reactionaries was inevitable. They shared the anti-intellectual assumption of the revolutionaries. The traditionalists attempted to restore the tradition without its intellectual life, just as the revolutionaries took as their assumption that man was alienated by finding himself in the Christian contemplative heaven. A commentator puts it thus:

> Revolution and the reaction from it to tradition and divine authority were forms of the same: the one the separation of human and divine, the other their immediate unity. The interest of subsequent theology, as of philosophy and the revolutionary culture generally, has been to recover the lost mediation.[96]

Let us consider part of how this recovery may occur in the English world. This brings us back to Dr Pusey and the Oxford Movement. Dr

Pusey, who died a century ago, was its biblical scholar; he was, from the age of twenty-eight until his death, Regius Professor of Hebrew in the University of Oxford. His appointment was deserved, as he had applied himself diligently to the acquisition of the appropriate philological learning. Having determined that English scholarship was inferior to German, he travelled to that country twice (at twenty-five and twenty-six) to obtain the best available there. He learned Arabic and Chaldee as well as Hebrew on what he subsequently regarded as the mistaken notion that the knowledge of the meaning of similar words in collateral languages would assist in discerning the meaning of Hebrew words.

While in Germany he discovered the development of the theological ideas and biblical criticism we have earlier explored. He wrote a two-part account of their nature together with a speculative analysis of their causes, his *An Historical Enquiry into the Probable Causes of the Rationalist Character lately Predominant in the Theology of Germany*. He regarded the results of this rationalism as mistaken and destructive. None the less consonant with his pietist-like principles, Dr Pusey hoped that this rationalism would have the effect of breaking down the orthodoxism into which German theology had ossified. That is, he hoped that the reduction of theology to rigid legal formularies might be overcome and produce a free Christianity inwardly felt and practical. He later repented this judgement as too optimistic and devoted his life to preventing the spread into England of the rationalist scholarship he had discovered in Germany. He even regretted having written the *Enquiry* on the ground that it provided information about these dangerous views and excited interest in them. This negative aspect of Dr Pusey's rearguard action expressed itself in the question of Dr Bloomfield, Bishop of London, who is said to have asked a candidate for Holy Orders: 'I trust, sir, that you do not understand German?'[97]

This approach did not work. People found out about German theology and, since the same spirit which produced it animated the utilitarian philosophy of the English, it proved irresistible. Indeed, the fuss made by the conservatives about *Essays and Reviews* helped draw attention to the ideas it contained and made the defence of them heroic and popular. Dr Pusey was not himself afraid of the notions; he knew they were dogmatically asserted and imported into Scripture. He was perfectly capable of showing how question begging they were as

81

presuppositions of biblical interpretation. In his published lectures on the Book of Daniel, he noted that dating the book after the events it prophesied was not justified on the mere ground that miraculous prophecy was impossible.[98] There was, however, no way of sweeping back the tide. Moreover, although Dr Pusey himself held that not the words but the doctrines were inspired and indeed such doctrines as had a decisively religious significance,[99] the conservatives were afraid to yield any ground at all, and defending too much, lost it all.[100] So Henry Liddon had to witness the head of Pusey House make biblical criticism acceptable to Anglican Catholics.

ASKING THE FATHERS

The negative programme did not succeed, but there was a more positive side to Dr Pusey's campaign against modern rationalism and biblical criticism: the restoration of patristic study. He devoted himself to resurrecting, popularizing, expositing and defending the theology of the Fathers and the older Anglican divines.[101] And indeed this is the only effective response to the end of the intellectual religion and institutional tradition announced and sought by the revolutionary philosophy, theology and praxis. The only way to discover and to prove that the old thinking is not a mere ideology of the past material circumstances of mankind, is to show it can govern our minds and hearts now, by thinking its intellectual content and directing ourselves in accord with the good thereby known. Since the end of our religious and secular culture comes about when modern man understands his being as sensuous and practical, we can only bring about the end of the end by becoming once more intellectual and spiritual beings.

Entering the tradition of the Fathers and the medieval doctors is an excellent place to start the recovery of a genuinely Christian biblical interpretation. Doubtless we must pass also to the Protestant Reformers, and to understand our current historical position we must find the way through modern and contemporary criticism, but the Fathers are necessary to the beginning. There are a number of ways they provide a new starting-point for biblical interpretation. First, the theology of the Fathers is profoundly intellectual in the broadest sense. They understood the Scripture through a high, speculative philosophy and through a coherent system of doctrine. The historical scholarship of liberalism and neo-orthodoxy has been incapable of properly appreciating the dialectic according to which, in the tradition, philosophical logic and scriptural revelation mutually developed while maintaining their integrity. Still, the tools are present for such an understanding. Secondly, the patristic and medieval treatment of Scripture predates the opposition of Scripture and tradition, which opposition is made the starting-point of the revolutionary criticism.[102] The result of this criticism is to turn the Bible into an instrument of the political theology of the contemporary Church; through the Fathers, on the contrary, we may learn how to unite the two with greater faithfulness to the objectivity of revelation. Finally, the earlier tradition precedes the excessive concentration on the question of the inspiration of Scripture. That is, the Fathers and the medieval doctors are not so much interested in the means by which revelation is present in Scripture. Rather, they teach that the essence of revelation is the raising of the mind of the biblical writers and of the hearers to grasp the intellectual content, the spiritual truth about God, his manner of working in us and his will for us, which it is the proper aim of Scripture to communicate.[103]

THE TIDE TURNS

A number of features of the current situation in biblical and theological study indicate that such a return to a patristic mode of looking at Scripture is part of what is happening. We may think of the union of Church and Scripture in the last stage of revolutionary theology, Brevard Child's treatment of the Bible from the standpoint of canonical form, an openness to considering earlier commentary when trying to discern the meaning of the text.[104] There is even an endeavour to re-establish the priority of Matthew as against Mark so as to restore faith in the integrity of the patristic tradition of the New Testament.[105] Unfortunately, much in this is one-sidedly anti-modern. Andrew Louth's *Discerning the Mystery* uses the extensions of Heidegger by H. G. Gadamer in order to reach over the nineteenth century, the Enlightenment and even beyond the Renaissance and Reformation to the ecclesiastical tradition. We shall not surmount the limitations of the Tractarian and Thomist revivals in this way.

Despite the real difficulties about the work of B. S. Childs, and the criticisms of him by James Barr, John Barton[106] and others,[107] his efforts to reunite Church and Scripture, dogmatic theology and the

Bible must be regarded as most serious, and more promising than those of Andrew Louth. B. S. Childs assumes and uses the work of critical scholarship and he actually employs his canonical approach in the interpretation of Scripture. Moreover, he wishes, in his reunifying efforts, to retain something of the Reformation determination to allow the Scripture sufficient independence so that Church and tradition are also judged by the Bible they possess, form and interpret. He falls thus into confusions such that John Barton can show that there are destructive ambiguities as to how the canonical approach combines literary and theological perspectives. Professor Barr successfully convicts Professor Childs of incoherently intermingling several senses of canon. But Professor Childs uses the criticisms to clarify and develop his method and he is endeavouring to unite more of the elements of any convincing reconstruction of our religious culture than are his opponents. Indeed, it is hopeful that the question is becoming clearer as our distance from the nineteenth century becomes greater. For it is promised that if we ask, we shall find, and it may be that we shall in our day be given our form of the answer.

NOTES

1 For the notion that our present situation is 'post-critical', see John Barton, *Reading the Old Testament: Method in Biblical Study* (London 1984), pp. 84, 95ff. Dr Barton as well as B. S. Childs, *The New Testament as Canon: An Introduction* (London 1984), pp. 35–7, 50–51, John Rogerson, *Old Testament Criticism in the Nineteenth Century: England and Germany* (London 1984), note 75, pp. 195–6, and 'Philosophy and the Rise of Biblical Criticism, England and Germany', S. W. Sykes (ed.), *England and Germany: Studies in Theological Diplomacy*, 'Studien zur interkulturellen Geschichte des Christentums', 25 (Frankfurt am Main/Bern 1982), pp. 75–6 and H. Graf von Reventlow, *The Authority of the Bible and the Rise of the Modern World* (London 1984), pp. 1–6 are variously concerned, after locating the cultural context or philosophical, theological, literary presuppositions of biblical criticism, either to find a place for it in reading the Scripture or to restore the context in which it appears normative or at least useful. My approach to it is as an historian of theology and especially of the history of the relation of theology to philosophy and culture generally – and indeed biblical criticism is increasingly being treated historically (historicizing the historicizers). Parts of this essay have been presented to audiences of very diverse sorts

in 1983 and 1984 including groups at Pusey House, Oxford; St Peter's Cathedral, Charlottetown, Prince Edward Island; the General Theological Seminary, New York City; St John's Church, Savannah, Georgia; the New Testament and Old Testament Seminars, Uppsala University, Sweden.

2 The Epistle is Romans 8.18–23, the Gospel is St Luke 6.36–42, the Collect reads: 'O God, the protector of all that trust in thee, without whom nothing is strong, nothing is holy; Increase and multiply upon us thy mercy; that, thou being our ruler and guide, we may so pass through things temporal, that we finally lose not the things eternal. Grant this, O heavenly Father, for Jesus Christ's sake.'

3 Making clear what it is we are looking for when we read the Bible as Scripture is perhaps our most difficult problem. John Barton, *Reading the Old Testament*, helps define the kinds of reading (and readers). He distinguishes from each other the pre-critical, the fundamentalist and the canonical (pp. 98–9), and is helpful on the relation between criticism and fundamentalism. Excursus III, 'The Canonical Approach and the "New Yale Theology"', (Childs, *The New Testament*, pp. 541–6) is the most recent theoretical statement on the question and his works are important attempts to read the Bible as Scripture. But other recent writers are at pains to reorient biblical studies on the ground that modern critical study has frequently failed to ask questions appropriate to the character of Scripture. An excellent collection of articles is John Rogerson (ed.), *Beginning Old Testament Study* (London 1983): 'It [the Old Testament] is not the national literature of the ancient Israelite people. It is a collection of religious books . . .' (p. 2). '. . . the Old Testament does not contain the history of ancient Israel. It contains historical and story-like traditions whose primary purpose is to express the faith of the authors of the OT that God has been involved in the events of the Israelite history. The material can be used by modern scholarship to reconstruct the history of Israel . . . Their primary purpose is not to provide source material for modern historians but to express faith in the God of Israel' (pp. 53 and 54). John Barton's essay 'Approaches to Ethics in the Old Testament', pp. 113–30, is useful on how to use the Bible as Scripture, as is John Rogerson's book *The Supernatural in the Old Testament* (Guildford and London 1976). The latter and his article in *Beginning* 'The World-View of the Old Testament' (pp. 55–73), are helpful in overcoming the positivistic bias of much critical and fundamentalist scholarship.

4 Cf., for example, Aristotle, *Metaphysica* I and XII; *Ethica Nico* I, VI, X; Genesis 2.2; Exodus 20.11; Luke 10.42; 1 Corinthians 13.12; 2 Corinthians 3.18; Hebrews 4.3ff.; 1 John 3.2. On our present partial knowledge of God: by reason, cf. Aristotle, *Metaphysica* I, 2; XII, 7; *Ethica Nico* X,8; by faith, cf. Hebrews 11 and 12.

5 Christopher Lind, 'Method in Contextual Theology', p. 14.

6 Cf. H. C. G. Matthew, 'Edward Bouverie Pusey: From Scholar to Tractarian', *Journal of Theological Studies*, n.s. XXXII, 1 (1981), pp. 101–24; but for a better view of Pusey showing the consistency of his anti-

rationalist views and purposes cf. R. D. Crouse, ' "Devout Perusal": The Tractarian Revival of Patristic Studies', a paper for the Ninth International Conference on Patristic Studies (Oxford 1983); idem, ' "Deepened by the Study of the Fathers": The Oxford Movement, Dr Pusey and Patristic Scholarship', *Dionysius* 7 (1983), pp. 137–47.

7 On the intellectual inadequacies of the reaction, cf. J. A. Doull, 'The Logic of Theology Since Hegel', *Dionysius* 7 (1983), pp. 129–36; R. D. Crouse's articles cited above, W. J. Hankey, 'Making Theology Practical: Thomas Aquinas and the Nineteenth-century Religious Revival', *Dionysius* 9 (1985), pp. 85–127. In the end the reactionaries were as anti-intellectual as the revolutionaries. The overcoming of the nineteenth century is a problem of restoring the primacy of intellect.

8 Cf. note 1 above.

9 All of this is treated with great subtlety and completeness by John Barton in *Reading the Old Testament*. He introduces the hermeneutic circle at pp. 5–6, the problem is concisely stated at p. 18. Ultimately he concludes that there are many possible and differing readings of the biblical text, that which one we adopt is a matter of intuition and that method can inform us of how we do read the text but not how we ought to read it. Dr Barton claims only theology can provide interpretative norms. Apart from a theological intervention, criticism ends then in endless subjectivity and scepticism (this last is my judgement of his conclusion, not John Barton's own) – cf. pp. 93–9 and 204–7.

10 Dr Barton maintains that the 'higher', 'lower' terminology is old-fashioned (p. 21).

11 J. Wellhausen, *Beilage zur Allgemeine Zeitung* (1908), p. 354, cited and translated by J. Rogerson, 'Philosophy and the Rise', p. 63.

12 On Marxism and structuralism, cf. *Reading the Old Testament*, pp. 122, 180–90; on what is involved in the shifts in the nineteenth and twentieth centuries from the perspectives of the author to that of the text and to that of the reader, consult the work as a whole. To discover the philosophical changes underlying these shifts, cf. A. Louth, *Discerning the Mystery* (Oxford 1983), pp. 32–3.

13 'Philosophy and the Rise', p. 64.

14 'Philosophy and the Rise', *passim*; *Old Testament Criticism*, p. 226.

15 *Old Testament Criticism*, p. 272.

16 On the national element in these reasonings, cf. Rogerson's article and book cited, R. Morgan, 'Historical Criticism and Christology: England and Germany', S. W. Sykes (ed.), *England and Germany*, pp. 80–112; J. Barton, *Reading the Old Testament*, pp. 161ff., and B. S. Childs, *The New Testament*, pp. 542ff. For Professor Rogerson it is crucial to re-educate the English student into more Germanic ways of thought in order to make biblical critical studies more effective: 'Philosophy and the Rise', pp. 75–6.

17 A. E. Harvey, *Jesus and the Constraints of History* (London 1982), p. 1.

18 C. S. Lewis, *Fern-seeds and Elephants and other essays on Christianity*, ed. Walter Hooper (Glasgow 1975), pp. 106–7. Lewis's statement is typical

of the reaction of the 'new criticism' emphasizing the 'text as it is' as against the 'personal heresy' of the author-oriented perspective which still dominated biblical criticism in Lewis's day. Biblical criticism seems to follow literary criticism at some distance; cf. J. Barton, *Reading the Old Testament*, pp. 178–9, 180ff., 154–6.

19 Lewis, *Fern-seeds*, p. 119.

20 D. F. Strauss, *The Life of Jesus critically examined*, translated from the fourth German edition, 3 vols. (London 1846) i, section 1.

21 The presuppositions of Sir Richard Jebb are much the same as those of Jowett; on Jowett's treatment of Plato see Ievan Ellis, *Seven against Christ, A Study of 'Essays and Reviews'* (Leiden 1980), p. 252. On Nietzsche cf. the introduction by Hugh Lloyd Jones to V. von Willamowitz-Moellendorff, *History of Classical Scholarship*, trans. A. Harris (London 1982), esp. pp. xi-xiii and his article in *Studies in Nietzsche and the Classical Tradition*, ed. O'Flaherty, Sellner and Helm (Univ. of North Carolina Press 1976); G. P. Grant, 'Nietzsche and the Ancients' Philosophy and Scholarship', *Dionysius* 3 (1979), pp. 5–16; and R. Friedrich, '*Euripidaristophanizein* and *Nietzschesokratizein*, Aristophanes, Nietzsche and the Death of Tragedy', *Dionysius* 4 (1980), pp. 5–36. Dr Friedrich concludes that Nietzsche's 'naturalism' renders 'his views of classical antiquity eccentric and often bizarre . . . they are hardly . . . a reliable guide for classical studies' (p. 36).

22 E. B. Pusey, *Daniel the Prophet: nine lectures delivered in the Divinity School of the University of Oxford*, 7th edition (London 1883), p. vi; see also pp. xi and xiii-xiv, cf. Ellis, op. cit., p. 125.

23 O. Chadwick, *The Victorian Church*, 2 vols. (London 1970), ii, p. 75.

24 H. P. Liddon, *The Divinity of Our Lord and Saviour Jesus Christ: eight lectures preached before the University of Oxford in the year 1866*, 7th edition (London, Oxford and Cambridge 1875), pp. 501ff. His judgements, though correct in principle, are not always accurate in their identification of the precise character of the philosophical presuppositions and political intentions of the critics. For example, he holds D. F. Strauss to be Hegelian philosophically and a social revolutionary in politics (pp. 501 and 502). Horton Harris, *David Friedrich Strauss and his Theology* (Cambridge, 1973) makes clear that by the time he wrote *Leben Jesu* Strauss was no longer a follower of Hegel (cf. pp. 76, 79ff., 136, 242, 270–71). See also his *Life of Jesus*, iii, sections 149–51. Strauss's unhappy political career (described by Harris, pp. 161–77) resulted from his election by radicals who drew conclusions from his theology which he did not himself draw. He remained strongly attached to a political and social order which would maintain a rather old-fashioned bourgeois culture. But even John Rogerson's *Old Testament Criticism* suffers from the fact that no one yet knows enough about both the history of philosophy and the history of biblical scholarship to bring them accurately together. For example, Rogerson designates Vatke's position as Hegelian (pp. 69–71), merely because of the idea of development but despite the fact that Vatke's notion of development would be dismissed as undialectical by

Hegel. Conversely, we may agree with Rogerson (p. 266) and von Reventlow (n. 6, p. 626) that Julius Wellhausen's position is not Hegelian without thereby concluding with Rogerson that his work is not philosophically determined.

25 Karl Marx, Frederick Engels, *Collected Works* (London 1975) iii, p. 175. Of Hegel and Strauss, Marx comments in his *Progress of Social Reform on the Continent*, iii, p. 404: 'Hegel . . . was so occupied with abstract questions that he neglected to free himself from the prejudices of his age – an age of restoration for old systems of government and religion . . . Hegel died in 1831 and as early as 1835 appeared Strauss's *Life of Jesus*, the first work showing some progress beyond the limits of orthodox Hegelianism.'

26 *Collected Works*, iii, pp. 354–7.

27 *The German Ideology, Collected Works*, v, p. 39.

28 (London 1828), pp. vi–vii.

29 *Economic and Philosophical Manuscripts of 1844*, Collected Works, iii, pp. 296–7.

30 This is the doctrine both of the *Meditations* and the *Discourses*.

31 Professor Doull puts the matter thus: 'The principle of this revolution is an individuality complete in its separation from the universal or ideal, which appears to it as mythical', art. cit., 129. For a more extended statement, cf. his 'Augustinian Trinitarianism and Existential Theology', *Dionysius* 3 (1979), pp. 111–59. To this difference between the anthropology of the Enlightenment and of the nineteenth-century revolution there corresponds a theological difference. The Enlightenment is typically Deist and, while God tends to become more remote and abstract, the 'Christian atheism' of the revolutionary theology is inconceivable. That is, it is inconceivable that God should disappear by becoming man which is the revolutionary solution to the *Deus absconditus* of the Enlightenment. On the character of Enlightenment theism see, most recently, John Macquarrie, *In Search of Deity: An Essay in Dialectical Theism* (London 1984), pp. 5–12.

32 Ludwig Feuerbach, *The Essence of Christianity*, trans. George Eliot, introduction by Karl Barth (Harper Torchbooks, New York 1957), iv, pp. 50 and 57.

33 *Old Testament Criticism*, pp. 24–5.

34 Cf. W. J. Hankey, 'Pope Leo's Purposes and St Thomas' Platonism', *Atti dell'VIII Congresso Tomistico Internazionale*, ed. A. Piolanti, 8 vols., viii, 'Studi Thomistici', (Citta del Vaticano 1982), pp. 39–52; idem, 'Aquinas' First Principle: Being and Unity?' *Dionysius* 4 (1980), pp. 133–72; idem, 'Making Theology Practical'.

35 On Pusey's attraction to Schleiermacher and to a moral emphasis in religion see H. P. Liddon, *Life of Edward Bouverie Pusey*, 4 vols., i (London 1893), pp. 82, 159, 166, 228; and on the whole matter R. D. Crouse, art. cit.

36 Eric Mascall, 'Whither Anglican Theology?', *When Will Ye Be Wise?*, ed. A. Kilmister (London 1983), p. 34. Dr Mascall is reporting with approval

the argument of S. W. Sykes, *The Integrity of Anglicanism* (Oxford 1978), pp. 21ff.

37 Cf. his *Principles of Christian Theology* (New York 1966), especially chapter IX, 'The Triune God'; J. A. Doull, 'Augustinian Trinitarianism and Existential Theology' contains a criticism.

38 Instructive on this point is the treatment of him in K. Barth, *Protestant Thought: From Rousseau to Ritschl*, translated from eleven chapters of *Die Protestantische Theologie im 19. Jahr hundert* (Zürich 1952; New York 1959).

39 A translation which includes a useful introductory essay on the relation of pietism and rationalism in the German Aufklärung is to be found in Harper Torchbooks (New York 1960). The introduction and translation are by Theodore M. Greene. Kant's argument for limiting reason to the ordering of sensation is found in his *Critique of Pure Reason*.

40 See, for example, *On the Genealogy of Morals*, Kaufmann trans. (New York 1969), III, 12, pp. 118–19 and *Joyful Wisdom*, Reinhardt trans. (New York 1960), IV, 335, pp. 259–63.

41 Rogerson, *Old Testament Criticism*, p. 49.

42 *Theodor*, i, p. 21; translated and quoted by Rogerson, ibid, p. 37.

43 See D. F. Strauss, *The Christ of Faith and the Jesus of History, A Critique of Schleiermacher's Life of Jesus* (Berlin 1865), trans. L. E. Kick, 'Lives of Jesus' (Philadelphia 1977); and also *Leben Jesu*, iii, 148 significantly entitled 'The eclectic Christology of Schleiermacher'.

44 *Theology in Germany*, i. p. 115, n; Liddon's consideration of Pusey's relation to Schleiermacher, *Life*, i, pp. 82ff. is most illumining.

45 Cf. Harris, *Strauss*, pp. 245–6.

46 Ibid., p. 99.

47 Ibid., p. 42; cf. also pp. 43, 204, 283.

48 Strauss, *Life of Jesus*, iii, p. 151.

49 Letter to Zeller, 6 November 1960 quoted in Harris, *Strauss*, p. 115. The complete chapter on Strauss and Baur in Harris is illumining on how biblical scholarship develops beyond Strauss.

50 See the Preface by Charles Gore to *Lux Mundi*, ed. Charles Gore (London 1889); see A. M. Ramsey, *From Gore to Temple* (London 1960) and note 22 above. For Liddon's reaction cf. J. O. Johnston, *Life and Letters of Henry Parry Liddon* (London 1904), pp. 360ff. On Lightfoot, etc., cf. S. Neill, *The Interpretation of the New Testament, 1861–1961* (London 1964); in general: my 'Making Theology Practical', J. Rogerson, *Old Testament Criticism*, pp. 209–19 and 273–89.

51 F. Temple, 'The Education of the World', *Essays and Reviews* (London 1860), p. 3.

52 Ibid., p. 44.

53 Ibid., p. 46.

54 Ibid., p. 47.

55 A. Schweitzer, *The Quest of the Historical Jesus*, 2nd English edn (London 1911), pp. 398–9.

56 A table setting out a 'Documentary Analysis of Genesis' may be found in

Peake's Commentary on the Bible, ed. M. Black (London 1962), p. 176.

57   Cf. J. Rogerson, 'An Outline of the History of Old Testament Study', in J. Rogerson (ed.), *Beginning Old Testament Study*, p. 20.

58   Cf. J. Rogerson, *Old Testament Criticism*, pp. 28–49, 69–78 and p. 272.

59   *Beginning Old Testament Study* seems to be greatly concerned with overcoming this orientation and arriving again at an understanding of what it would mean to regard the Old Testament as Scripture, cf. note 3 above. Wellhausen resigned his theology chair because he found his researches incompatible with preparing clergy, cf. R. Smend, 'Julius Wellhausen and his *Prolegomena to the History of Israel*', in *Julius Wellhausen and His 'Prolegomena to the History of Israel*', ed. D. A. Knight, Semeia 25 (Chicago 1982), p. 6.

60   Rogerson, *An Outline*, pp. 20–21.

61   Cf. *The Genealogy of Morals*, parts I and III.

62   J. Wellhausen, *Prolegomena to the History of Israel*, trans. Black and Menzies, (Edinburgh 1885), p. 412 as quoted by Smend, art. cit., p. 14. Cf. also D. A. Knight, 'Wellhausen and the Interpretation of Israel's Literature', in Knight (ed.), pp. 21–36 esp. 26, and 30–33.

63   Schweitzer's own position is not far from this.

64   Cf. R. Bultmann, *Jesus Christ and Mythology* (New York 1958), pp. 45–59, and J. Macquarrie, *An Existentialist Theology, A Comparison of Heidegger and Bultmann* (London 1955). The first pages of Professor Macquarrie's book (esp. pp. 16ff.) contain a presentation of the Old Testament 'biblical theologians' such as Wright and Eichrodt, so that it appears how they operate within the same general philosophic framework as Bultmann.

65   Bultmann, op. cit., p. 84.

66   Ibid., p. 31, cf. also pp. 40–41.

67   Ibid., p. 19.

68   Macquarrie, *An Existentialist Theology*, p. 185.

69   Bultmann's position is in philosophic principle the same as that of Karl Rahner, cf. *Spirit in the World*, trans. from 2nd German edn by W. Dych (London 1968), pp. 407–8.

70   A. Phillips, *Lower Than the Angels* (Oxford 1983), p. x; also pp. 64–5.

71   James Barr, *The Semantics of Biblical Language* (Oxford 1961), p. 13.

72   Ibid., *passim*; B. S. Childs, *Biblical Theology in Crisis* (Philadelphia 1970); J. Barr, *Holy Scripture: Canon Authority, Criticism* (Oxford 1983), esp. Appendix III, pp. 130–71; J. Barton, 'Old Testament Theology', *Beginning Old Testament Study*, pp. 90–112.

73   B. S. Childs, *Biblical Theology in Crisis*, pp. 16, 56, 110; Barr, *Holy Scripture*, pp. 140ff.; J. Barton, *Reading*, pp. 208–11.

74   Cf. M. Heidegger, 'The Onto-theo-logical Constitution of Metaphysics', *Identity and Difference*, trans. J. Stambaugh (New York 1969).

75   Barth, 'An Introductory Essay', to Feuerbach, *The Essence* (see note 32 above), p. xxiv. For a similar judgement of Feuerbach, cf. Barth's *Protestant Thought*, pp. 357–9. Of equal importance is the degree to which Barth allows Kant to set the terms within which modern theology

can proceed, ibid., pp. 188–96.

76 Barth, 'An Introductory Essay', p. xxv.

77 Cf. J. Moltmann, *Theology of Hope*, trans. J. W. Leitch (London 1967), pp. 168ff.; idem, *The Trinity and the Kingdom of God*, trans. M. Kohl (London 1981), pp. 139ff. J. Sobrino, *Christology at the Crossroads, A Latin-American Approach*, trans. J. Brury (London 1981), pp. 22–33.

78 Sobrino, op. cit., pp. 27–32 and Lind, art. cit., but see Moltmann, *Trinity*, pp. 192–3, against a reflection theory of the role of religion in history.

79 J. Moltmann, *Religion, Revolution and the Future*, trans M. D. Meeks (New York 1969), p. 77.

80 Ibid., p. 51; cf. also Moltmann, *The Crucified God*, trans. R. A. Wilson and J. Bowden (London 1974), pp. 166ff.; idem, *Theology*, pp. 172ff.

81 Idem, *Religion*, p. 51.

82 Idem, *Theology*, p. 179.

83 Moltmann, *Trinity*, pp. 191–2.

84 Moltmann, *Crucified*, p. 317.

85 On these developments cf. Monica Furlong (ed.), *Feminine in the Church* (London 1984) and William Oddie, *What will happen to God? Feminism and the Reconstruction of Christian Belief* (London 1984).

86 Cf. Moltmann, *Trinity*, chapter VI and W. Pannenberg, *Basic Questions in Theology: collected essays*, trans. G. H. Kehm, 3 vols. (London 1970–71), iii, pp. 6 and 7.

87 J. Barton, *Reading*, p. 207.

88 Four vols. (Chicago and London 1957). The situation with Old Testament scholarship was not the same so long as the biblical theology movement survived. Cf. Childs, *The Crisis in Biblical Theology*.

89 This has already begun even in Canada! See the contributions to the Anglicans in Mission 'Background Papers' by the Revd Carl Major, Development Education Secretary, Anglican Church of Canada, and by the Revd Cyril Powles, Professor of Church History at Trinity College, Toronto. Christopher Lind, author of 'Method in Contextual Theology' also taught at Trinity. The liturgy, together with suggestions for its use and for the sermon accompanying it produced by the National Liturgical Officer of the ACC for Anglicans in Mission Sunday, 14 November 1982, is a perfect example of the transformation of biblical eschatology into revolutionary praxis. Cf. also M. Rumscheidt's Address quoted above, A. Van Seters, 'Social Hermeneutics', in *ARC*, a publication of the theological community of the Faculty of Religious Studies of McGill University, its affiliated Colleges, and the Montreal Institute for Ministry, X (1982), I, pp. 11–19 and the Report of the Sixteenth Atlantic Ecumenical Conference, 1981 ed. by M. R. B. Lovesey.

90 Rumscheidt, 'Address'.

91 *Reading*, p. 207.

92 In addition to the works of these authors cited, see Ernest Nicholson, *Interpreting the Old Testament, A Century of the Oriel Professorship* (Oxford 1981).

93   *The Authority of the Bible*, p. 6.

94   See especially Childs, *The New Testament*, on this as the critical problem: particularly pp. 21, 35–47, 541–6. At p. 541 he praises G. A. Lindbeck's *The Nature of Doctrine. Religion and Theology in a Postliberal Age* (Philadelphia 1984) and other products of the 'New Yale theology' because 'any attempt to narrow the wide gap between dogmatic theology and biblical studies should be encouraged'. Cf. also note 1 above and A. Louth, *Discerning the Mystery*.

95   A brief treatment of the current situation of Catholic biblical scholarship may be found in R. E. Brown *et al.* (eds.), *The Jerome Biblical Commentary* (Englewood Cliffs 1968). The dedication to Pope Pius XII and the Foreword are instructive as to the preliminaries to the second Vatican Council.

96   J. A. Doull, 'The Logic of Theology since Hegel', p. 133.

97   Ellis, *Seven*, p. 7.

98   Pusey, op. cit., preface.

99   Liddon, *Life*, i, pp. 184–5.

100 Cf. Owen Chadwick, *The Victorian Church*, on the causes of the rigidity and defensiveness of Victorian Christianity, on Liddon especially, ii, pp. 101ff.

101 Cf. Crouse, 'Devout Perusal' and 'Deepened by the Study' and A. Louth, 'The Oxford Movement, the Fathers and the Bible', *Sobornost*, 6 (1984), pp. 1, 30–45.

102 Cf. Andrew Louth, *Discerning the Mystery* (Oxford 1982).

103 Cf. for example, Thomas Aquinas, *Summa Theologiae*, I, 1, 8 *ad* 2; I, 12, 11 *ad* 2. Vision of God '*in sua essentia*' is the ground of revelation and is given to Moses and Paul, *ST*, II–II, 175, 3 *ad* 1.

104 But see Barr's criticism, *Holy Scripture*, Appendix III.

105 Cf. J. F. A. Sawyer, 'A change in emphasis in the study of the prophets', *Israel's Prophetic Tradition, Essays in Honour of Peter R. Ackroyd* (Cambridge 1982), pp. 234 and 243.

106 Cf. James Barr, *Holy Scripture*, Appendix III, J. Barton, *Reading*, pp. 77–103, 208–11. B. Childs, *The New Testament*, pp. 22–7, 541–6.

107 For example, B. Orchard, B. and T. Longstaff, *J. J. Griesbach: Synoptic and Text-critical Studies, 1776–1976* (Cambridge 1979); William R. Farmer (ed.), *New Synoptic Studies: The Cambridge Gospel Conference and Beyond*, (Mercer University Press 1983); B. Orchard and H. Riley, *Order in the Synoptics*, (Mercer University Press 1985).

2 Not in the Wisdom of Men

ROGER BECKWITH

How far can the 'wisdom of men' be trusted? If modern theology has reached a dead end, is it because it has trusted merely human wisdom too much? Is there a reasonably clear and consistent biblical teaching on the relationship between human understanding and God's own self-disclosure? How *is* wisdom to be gained?

THE BEGINNING OF WISDOM

In the ancient world, wisdom (the *hokmah* of the Hebrew Bible and the *sophia* of the Greek) was one of the most greatly esteemed goods of mankind. Both Mesopotamian and Egyptian texts bearing the names of wise men and recording their wisdom have been discovered, such as the *Wisdom of Amenophis*, which has links with a passage in the biblical Book of Proverbs.[1] In Solomon's dream at the beginning of his reign, in which the Lord invites him to ask what he will, the goods which he could have asked are listed as length of days, riches for himself or the life of his enemies; instead of any of which he asks for a wise and understanding heart to judge his people (1 Kings 3; 2 Chron. 1). God grants his request, and as a result he is compared to his advantage with all the wise men of surrounding countries:

> God gave Solomon wisdom and understanding exceeding much . . . Solomon's wisdom excelled all the wisdom of the children of the east, and all the wisdom of Egypt, for he was wiser than all men, than Ethan the Ezrahite, and Heman and Calcol and Darda the sons of Mahol: and his fame was in all the nations round about (1 Kings 4.29–31).[2]

It was wisdom which rulers needed for their task, just as it was wisdom which craftsmen needed for theirs. The practical skills of Bezalel and Oholiab and the rest of those who constructed the tabernacle and its furnishings are likewise described, in the Book of Exodus, as a wisdom put into their hearts by the Lord (Exod. 28.3; 31.3, 6; 35.26, 31; 36.1f.). In the pagan world, wisdom was deemed to include cultic skills and magic, and was regarded as a gift from pagan deities, but in the Old Testament those who truly receive wisdom from the true God are always found wiser than their pagan rivals. 'Now therefore let Pharaoh look out a man discreet and wise,' says Joseph, and receives the reply, 'Forasmuch as God has showed thee all this, there is none so discreet and wise as thou' (Gen. 41.33-9). Similarly, when 'God gave knowledge and skill in all learning and wisdom' to Daniel and his companions, 'they were found ten times better in every matter of wisdom and understanding than all the magicians and enchanters that were in all his [i.e. Nebuchadnezzar's] realm' (Dan. 1.17,20).

Solomon's wisdom, whatever its limitations, seems to have extended well outside the skills of government (1 Kings 4.33; 10.1-3), and the specific 'wisdom literature' of the Old Testament, in which Solomon's is one of the greatest names, concerns itself much less with the demands of particular roles in life than with the human condition in general, and with ultimate questions of life and death, God and man.[3] This literature lays down the principle that wisdom is ultimately a property of the Lord himself:

> With him is wisdom and might;
> He hath counsel and understanding (Job 12.13).

For this reason, wisdom is primarily located in God's providential governing of nature and mankind (Job 12.13-25), and indeed in his original creation of them (Prov. 3.19; 8.22-31). But, as Proverbs 8 goes on to say, this wisdom which is the Creator's own prerogative is available also to men, if they are willing to receive it. For 'the Lord giveth wisdom' (Prov. 2.6), or, as Daniel, which has many of the qualities of wisdom literature,[4] puts it,

> Wisdom and might are his . . . he giveth wisdom unto the wise,
> and knowledge to them that know understanding (Dan. 2.20f.).

Solomon's wisdom, as we saw, was given to him by the Lord, and so was Bezalel's and Oholiab's, Joseph's and Daniel's. And this is the general principle, that wisdom is the Lord's prerogative, and that he is the giver of it. Such teaching, once established, continues through into the New Testament also, where James says:

> If any of you lack wisdom, let him ask of God, who giveth to all liberally and upbraideth not (Jas. 1.5),

and where Paul prays that God

> may give unto you a spirit of wisdom and revelation in the knowledge of him (Eph. 1.17).

To receive wisdom from God requires a willingness to renounce one's own wisdom:

> Trust in the Lord with all thine heart,
> *And lean not upon thine own understanding;*
> In all thy ways acknowledge him,
> And he shall direct thy paths.
> *Be not wise in thine own eyes;*
> Fear the Lord, and depart from evil (Prov. 3.5–7).

Similarly Daniel, after saying that it is God who gives wisdom to the wise, adds the disclaimer, 'this secret is not revealed to me for any wisdom that I have more than any living' (Dan. 2.30); and the emphasis is once again carried through into the New Testament, for example in Paul's warnings, 'lest ye be wise in your own conceits . . . Be not wise in your own conceits' (Rom. 11.25; 12.16). The prophet Isaiah speaks similarly (Isa. 5.21), and Jeremiah's warning to wise men against boasting is to the same effect:

> Thus saith the Lord, *Let not the wise man glory in his wisdom*, neither let the mighty man glory in his might, nor let the rich man glory in his riches, but let him that glorieth glory in this, that he understandeth and knoweth me, that I am the Lord, who exercise loving-kindness, judgement and righteousness in the earth: for in these things I delight, saith the Lord (Jer. 9.23f.).

But if true wisdom comes from God, and to receive it involves knowing him, trusting in him with all one's heart and renouncing one's own wisdom, it follows that 'the fear of the Lord is the beginning of wisdom'. This principle is laid down in Proverbs and in Job. Proverbs says,

The fear of the Lord is the beginning of wisdom,
And the knowledge of the Holy One is understanding (Prov. 9.10).

In the same way, Job concludes his inquiry where wisdom may be found, by declaring

Behold, the fear of the Lord, that is wisdom,
And to depart from evil is understanding (Job 28.28).

The principle is also echoed in one of the Psalms (Ps. 111.10), a number of which reflect wisdom-teaching. The term 'fear' (*yirah*) should be noted, since it implies that not just faith but repentance, and the obedience which follows from it, are basic to true wisdom. The 'knowledge of the *Holy One*' cannot leave a man indifferent to his holiness, but creates in him 'fear' and causes him to 'depart from evil'. The moral implications of wisdom are also evident in the quotations made from Proverbs 3.5–7 and Jeremiah 9.23f. in the previous paragraph, and in Daniel 12.10:

None of the *wicked* shall understand,
But they that be wise shall understand:

and once again the teaching is carried on into the New Testament, where we read of 'the wisdom of the *righteous*' (Luke 1.17), and where James expands on the matter at length:

Who is wise and understanding among you? Let him show by his *good life* his works in *meekness* of wisdom. But if ye have bitter jealousy and faction in your heart, boast not and lie not against the truth. This wisdom is not that which cometh down from above, but is earthly, sensual, devilish. For where jealousy and faction are, there is confusion and every vile deed. But the wisdom that is from above is first *pure*, then *peaceable, gentle, easy to be entreated, full of mercy and good fruits*, without variance, without hypocrisy (Jas. 3.13–17).[5]

With the truly wise man, who knows God and therefore fears him, the wisdom literature regularly contrasts the fool (*kesil, nabal, ewil, sakal*), but it is in the Psalms that the contrast is most sharply stated. The fool 'says in his heart, There is no God', and therefore does 'abominable works' (Pss. 14.1; 53.1). In the New Testament, Paul extends this analysis from atheists to idolaters, who have perverted the truth about God rather than wholly denying it. Idolaters, too, though 'professing themselves to be wise, have become fools', because they 'hold down the truth in unrighteousness', and are therefore 'given up by God to a reprobate mind, to do those things which are not fitting' (Rom. 1.18-32).

How God mediates the wisdom which he gives is not a point on which wisdom literature says a great deal. Proverbs 2.6 implies that he mediates it by his words:

> The Lord giveth wisdom:
> *Out of his mouth* cometh knowledge and understanding.

The primary form of such words might be proverbs, such as are specifically named in Ecclesiastes, where we read that

> Because the Preacher was *wise*, he still taught the people knowledge; yea, he pondered, and sought out, and set in order many *proverbs*. The Preacher sought to find out acceptable words, and that which was written uprightly, even words of truth. The words of the *wise* are as goads, and as nails well fastened are the words of the collections of sentences, which are given from One Shepherd (Eccles. 12.9-11).[6]

However, any form of divine discourse which conveyed wisdom would qualify to be ranked with the proverbs which the divine 'Shepherd' gave, and there are passages in the Old Testament which make such a claim both for the Law and for prophecy. Of the Law, we read

> Behold, I have taught you *statutes and judgements*, even as the Lord my God commanded me, that ye should do so in the midst of the land whither ye go in to possess it. Keep therefore and do them; for this is *your wisdom and your understanding* in the sight of the peoples, which shall hear all these statutes, and say, Surely this great nation is a *wise and understanding* people (Deut. 4.5f.).

And,

> *Thy commandments* make me *wiser* than my enemies . . .
> I have *more understanding* than all my teachers,
> For *thy testimonies* are my meditation.
> I *understand more* than the aged
> Because I have kept *thy precepts* (Ps. 119.98-100).

97

And of prophecy,

> Who is *wise*, and he shall understand these things? prudent, and he shall know them? (Hos. 14.9; cf. Jer. 9.12; Dan. 12.10).

In the New Testament likewise, Jesus concludes the Sermon on the Mount by speaking of his own teaching in a similar manner:

> Everyone therefore who heareth *these words of mine*, and doeth them, shall be likened unto a *wise man*, who built his house upon the rock. . . And everyone that heareth these words of mine, and doeth them not, shall be likened unto a foolish man, who built his house upon the sand (Matt. 7.24–27).

WISE MEN AND BABES

As we saw at the beginning of this essay, the Old Testament compares Solomon, Joseph and Daniel, to their advantage, with the wise men of other nations. Because their wisdom came from the Lord, it excelled any merely human sagacity. In Israel also, however, there were some 'wise men' who were more crafty than godly, and who, because of their influence at court and elsewhere, sometimes came into conflict with the prophets. Isaiah, when condemning the superficiality of the national religion of his day, gives the warning:

> I will proceed to do a marvellous work among this people, even a marvellous work and a wonder: and the wisdom of their wise men shall perish, and the understanding of their prudent men shall be hid (Isa. 29.14).

Jeremiah, likewise, condemns the unfaithfulness of wise men, alongside that of priests and prophets:

> The wise men are ashamed, they are dismayed and taken: lo, they have rejected the word of the Lord; and what manner of wisdom is in them? (Jer. 8.9).

In rejecting the word of the Lord, they had rejected wisdom.

We noted on p. 95 the insistence that, in order to receive wisdom from God, a willingness to renounce one's own wisdom is required. For the 'wise man', whose natural tendency was to 'glory in his wisdom' (Jer. 9.23), this was a hard lesson. Nevertheless, it was a lesson which needed to be learned, for one could not 'trust in the Lord', and his wisdom, 'with all one's heart', but at the same time 'lean upon one's own understanding'. And since, as we saw on p. 97f., God's wisdom was mediated through what he said (whether proverb, law or prophecy), to trust in him meant to trust in his word. Conversely, to reject his word, as Jeremiah pointed out (Jer. 8.9), was to reject wisdom itself.

After the destruction of the monarchy, the wise man of the royal court lost his importance in Israel, but the name 'wise man' became attached instead to those scribes or elders who, some time after the Exile, took over from the priests and Levites the duty of teaching God's law to the people.[7] In the rabbinical literature, the Pharisaic scholars are sometimes called *sopherim* (scribes), sometimes *zekenim* or *sabim* (elders), and sometimes also *hakamim* (wise men, sages); but the three titles are already used more or less interchangeably by Ben Sira in Ecclesiasticus, written not later than about 180 BC: and it is to people of this class that the title 'wise man' would have been applied in the time of Jesus.

The wise men of the intertestamental and New Testament period were not *worldly*-wise. They acknowledged that wisdom came from God and was found in his word; and, with the decline of oral prophecy, and following the lead given by Ezra, they increasingly concentrated their attention to God's word on the Pentateuch and the other written Scriptures. In more subtle ways, however, they failed to be guided by the Scriptures, following a tradition of interpretation which laid special stress on the outward regulations of tithing and ceremonial cleanness (Matt. 23.23-8; Luke 11.39-42).[8] As Jesus pointed out, this made it possible to neglect the weightier matters of the Law, judgement, mercy and faith, and to put outward cleanness before cleanness of the heart: hence his constant charge of hypocrisy against them. It also placed obedience to the Law within the power of man, and so encouraged self-righteousness (Luke 10.29; 18.9). Jesus challenged their tradition of interpretation, and he challenged their pride, and this was what made them so resistant to his own teaching and so hostile to himself.

Nothing is more characteristic of the teaching of Jesus than his emphasis on humility (on not exalting oneself) and on faith (on not being anxious, since we have a heavenly Father). Nor is anything more striking than the frequency with which he sets a child before his hearers as an example: they must 'humble themselves as this little child' (Matt. 18.4), they must become one of 'the little ones that believe on me' (Mark 9.42). This was the right approach to God, and to his word the Scriptures; and it was also, Jesus claimed, the right approach to himself, and to his own teaching.

A saying which occurs in the Gospels of Matthew and Luke contrasts the reaction he encountered from the little ones that believed on him to the reaction of the wise men of his day:

> I thank thee, O Father, Lord of heaven and earth, that thou didst hide these things from the wise and understanding, and didst reveal them unto babes: yea, Father, for so it was well pleasing in thy sight (Matt. 11.25f.; Luke 10.21).[9]

Because of their different reactions, the 'babes' had received the privilege of the revelation of the Father through Jesus of which the next verse speaks, but the wise men had not. The babes thus became the truly wise men. As Jesus says in the Fourth Gospel,

> For judgement came I into this world, that they which see not may see; and that they which see may become blind (John 9.39),

or as Simeon foretold at his birth,

> Behold, this child is set for the falling and rising up of many in Israel, and for a sign which is spoken against . . . that thoughts out of many hearts may be revealed (Luke 2.34f.).

The 'wise men' of Israel (though this time religious wise men), in rejecting the word of the Lord through Jesus, were just as surely rejecting God's wisdom as were their ancestors who 'rejected the word of the Lord' through Jeremiah. And the reason was much the same, that they were 'glorying in their wisdom' and 'leaning upon their own understanding', instead of humbling themselves to put their trust in the wisdom of God. They were also forgetting the moral demands of wisdom, that its beginning is 'the fear of the Lord'. With pride and hatred in their hearts, they would not and could not recognize the teaching of Jesus for what it was. A moral conversion was needed. But, as Jesus said,

> If any man *willeth to do his* (God's) *will*, he shall know of the teaching, whether it be of God, or whether I speak from myself (John 7.17).

Those who had humbled themselves before God as little children could meet this requirement of 'willing to do his will', but there was no other way of meeting it.

THE FOOLISHNESS OF GOD AND THE WISDOM OF MEN

The opening three chapters of Paul's First Epistle to the Corinthians (beginning at 1 Cor. 1.17) are like a summary of the teaching of the Old Testament and the teaching of Jesus on divine and human wisdom.[10] Once again, the contrast between the two is strongly drawn, the one depending on divine revelation, the other on man's own resources; and likewise the opposition to one another in which they constantly stand, each rejecting the other as really foolishness (1 Cor. 1.18–27; 2.14; 3.18f.), though Paul, in an ironical way, at times accepts the description of 'foolishness' for what is actually wisdom. God's threat of judgement on worldly wisdom in Isaiah 29.14 and his warning to the wise man against boasting in Jeremiah 9.23f., which we discussed on pp. 98, 95, are both here quoted (1 Cor. 1.19, 31; cf. verses 26–9). The wise men of contemporary Judaism, who opposed Jesus, are considered (1 Cor. 1.20, 22f.), as well as the wise men of the pagan world; and the gospel comparison of believers with babes is echoed (1 Cor. 3.1). Yet in various respects matters are carried further.

In the first place, addressed as the epistle is to Corinth, it is the wise men of Greece (i.e. the philosophers and sophists) who become the characteristic wise men of the pagan world, in the place of the wise men of Egypt and Babylon, known to Joseph, Solomon and Daniel. Yet, for all their culture and intelligence, the wise men of Greece are seen to represent a merely human wisdom, which therefore fares no better than that of Egypt and Babylon in comparison with the revealed wisdom of God.

Secondly, the distinction between the wise men of Judaism and the wise men of Greece is specified as the distinction between those who demand 'signs' (*miraculous* proofs) and those who demand 'wisdom' (*rational* proofs). Neither, however, are willing to humble themselves to *believe* (1 Cor. 1.21–4).

Thirdly, writing in the wake of Calvary and Pentecost, Paul's message is centred not simply upon Christ, but upon Christ crucified, and is much more explicit than any earlier wisdom teaching with regard to the activity of the Holy Spirit. In the message of Christ crucified, the wisdom of God comes to its climax:

> We preach Christ crucified, unto Jews a stumbling-block, and unto Gentiles *foolishness*, but unto them that are called, both Jews and Greeks, Christ the power of God and the *wisdom* of God (1 Cor. 1.23f.; cf. 1.18–21; 2.2).

Also, the Holy Spirit is active in this preaching, both in inspiring the apostles' words (1 Cor. 2.6–13) and in moving their hearers to receive their message as the true wisdom (1 Cor. 2.4f., 14–16):

> We received not the spirit of the world, but the Spirit which is of God; that we might know the things that are freely given to us by God. Which things also we speak, not in words which *man's wisdom* teacheth, but which the Spirit teacheth . . . Now the natural man receiveth not the things of the Spirit of God; for they are *foolishness* unto him . . . But he that is spiritual judgeth all things . . .

Fourthly, Paul develops Jesus's image of believers as 'babes' in a significant way. He contrasts them with the 'full-grown' (1 Cor. 2.6). When Paul had come to evangelize Corinth, he had determined to renounce Greek rhetoric and Greek wisdom, and to depend simply on the message of the cross and the power of the Holy Spirit (1 Cor. 2.1–5). When he now writes, the Corinthians are still babes, capable only of receiving milk, not solid food (1 Cor. 3.1–3). However, there is evidently solid food available for 'full-grown' or 'mature' Christians: 'howbeit we speak wisdom among the full-grown' (1 Cor. 2.6). But as soon as he has said this, he safeguards his words against any idea that he is now dispensing with the cross and introducing Greek philosophy by the back door. For he goes on:

> Yet a wisdom *not of this world* . . . but we speak *God's wisdom in a mystery*, even the wisdom *that hath been hidden*, which God foreordained before the worlds unto our glory . . . *Things which eye saw not, and ear heard not, and which entered not into the heart of man*, whatsoever things God prepared for them that love him. But *unto us God revealed them through the Spirit*: for the Spirit searcheth all things, yea, the deep things of God (1 Cor. 2.6–10).

Hence, this more advanced Christian teaching is just as much grounded in revelation as is the elementary teaching. It is God's wisdom, not man's; it is hidden, consisting of truths which have not been seen, heard or even thought of; and it is only known to Christians because God has revealed it through the Holy Spirit. What this more advanced teaching is, Paul does not tell the immature Corinthians except perhaps in one particular: the word 'mystery' (*musterion*, secret) recurs in 1 Corinthians 15.51, and is there used of a specific revelation about the way that the final resurrection will take place, which follows in verses 51-7. The word is also used of specific truths, and not simply of the Gospel in general, in the Epistles to the Ephesians and Colossians (in the former several times): and if those twin Epistles do concentrate on Paul's more advanced teaching, that would help to explain the different character they have, when compared with his other Epistles.[11] Outside Paul's writings, but within his circle probably, the distinction between the 'milk' and the 'solid food' of the Gospel reappears in Hebrews 5.11—6.3. Hebrews aims to provide the latter, and once again the complete dependence of this advanced teaching on revelation is clear. For the Epistle mainly consists of exegesis of the Old Testament, and deductions drawn from that exegesis, in support and illustration of the apostolic teaching about Jesus.[12]

REFLECTIONS ON THE RECENT HISTORY OF THEOLOGY

Those who have had the patience to follow this essay thus far, will have observed that it lays stress on the unity rather than the diversity of biblical teaching about wisdom. The writer has made a conscious effort not to neglect the diverse settings in which this teaching is found, or the special emphases of the Old Testament wisdom literature, Jesus and Paul, nor to impose an artificial unity upon them, in the way that the once-fashionable Biblical Theology movement and Conservative Evangelicalism have been rather prone to do. Nevertheless, if only because later parts of the biblical literature tend to assume and to build upon earlier parts, and in this matter clearly do, the wisdom teaching which we have been looking at has a very strongly marked unity.

One of its constant emphases has been on the radical difference between human wisdom and divine, and on the moral conversion from

103

pride to humility and faith which is needed if one is to move from the former to the latter. This does not mean that divine wisdom is of a non-intellectual character, as is sufficiently shown by the repeated stress on 'understanding' which we find. A variety of words for 'understanding' are used in the Book of Proverbs, and occur there over fifty times; and Jesus and Paul are no less emphatic on the matter. To love God with all the 'mind' (*dianoia*) or all the 'understanding' (*sunesis*), so Jesus teaches, is part of the first and great commandment (Mark 12.30, 33). And Paul's polemic against a spirituality which bypassed the 'mind' (*nous*) and the 'understanding' (*phrenes*) in 1 Corinthians 14.1–25 is to the same effect, as is his positive teaching about the role of the understanding elsewhere. 'Wisdom' and 'understanding' are therefore often explicitly linked, both in the Old Testament wisdom literature (Prov. 2.6; 4.5; 8.1; 10.13, 23 etc.) and in Paul (Eph. 1.8; Col. 1.9), and it is clear that to receive the divine wisdom is to have one's understanding enlightened.

Since the understanding is needed for the apprehension of divine wisdom, it is natural that the understanding is also active in following out the consequences of divine wisdom. When the Lord answers Job out of the whirlwind, and points to the inscrutability of his activities in nature as an analogy explaining the inscrutability of his activities in providence (Job 38—41), this is an intellectual argument, addressed to the understanding. The same is the case when Jesus points to God's provision of the needs of the lower creation as evidence that he will also provide the needs of his human children (Matt. 6.25–33), or when Paul argues from the truth of the empty tomb to show that the future bodily resurrection of other men is not impossible either (1 Cor. 15. 12–23). The application by Jesus of the moral principles laid down in Scripture to actual situations (Matt. 4.4, 7; Mark 7.9–13, etc.), and the application by Paul of the doctrinal principles laid down in Scripture to the combating of contemporary errors (Rom. 4; Gal. 3, etc.), are once again intellectual arguments, addressed to the understanding.

The challenge which revelation issues to human wisdom is not, therefore, anything like an invitation to intellectual suicide. Instead, it is an invitation to exercise one's mind on *new truth*, unavailable apart from revelation. From this point of view, it is more like intellectual suicide to content oneself with philosophical empiricism, of the sort that has been popular since the time of Hume, and to assert that anything outside ordinary human experience is either unreliable or false; for by such a decision one denies oneself the whole intellectual activity which is theology. For theology is an intellectual activity, but it proceeds from revelation and therefore from faith. As Anselm's famous words put it, *Credo ut intelligam*, 'I believe, in order that I may understand' (*Proslogion* 1).

The Reformation, as Colin Brown has said,[13] was a reassertion of Anselm's approach. Arising in the context of the Renaissance of learning, it attempted to harness the new learning to the service of the faith of the Bible. The Enlightenment of the eighteenth century attempted, in one important respect, to carry this programme further. By pioneering the historical approach to the Bible, it taught the Church to see the Bible against the background of ancient contemporary conditions and cultures, which were then beginning to be investigated in all their variety, and not to see it in a vacuum or as an undifferentiated whole.[14] This was an achievement of permanent value, which is all the time being developed further. Unfortunately, however, the influence of non-Christian philosophy had by the eighteenth century already started to make deep inroads into theological thought. Neither then or since, of course, did most theologians capitulate completely to such philosophy, but they allowed it to compromise their theology and to sap their faith. Whether the philosophy in vogue since that time has been the rationalism of Wolff, the empiricism of Hume, the moralism of Kant or the idealism of Hegel, it has in each case proceeded from a subjective and humanistic starting-point, which necessarily excluded the Bible as a source of objective revelation. And since the Deists had already set the example of boldly rejecting the Bible in favour of their own natural religion, or only accepting from it selectively ideas which could be supported on grounds quite alien to itself, the men of the Enlightenment felt free to do the same in the interests of their own chosen philosophy. As a result, an attitude of scepticism towards the Bible became the norm among theologians in eighteenth-century Germany,[15] and later became common elsewhere.

It is not the task of this essay, as it was of that preceding it, to trace the course of the philosophical rewritings of biblical history which followed in the Germany of the nineteenth and twentieth centuries, though every major theological trend which we have experienced in the English-speaking world (whether a paler reflection or a reaction) has probably had its source there. From this point of view, the *Tracts for the Times* were an attempt to go back behind German biblical criticism to the authority of tradition, *Essays and Reviews* was a proposal to embrace such criticism wholeheartedly, *Lux Mundi* was an effort to salvage the creed while sacrificing nearly everything else, and other inconsistent compromises have been tried since.[16] Instead, our theme here has been the contrast, regularly drawn in biblical teaching, between the divine wisdom of revelation, known only to humble faith, and self-sufficient human wisdom, which is really foolishness. And the question with which we must end is whether it is not true that the Church has, over the last two centuries, continually allowed the latter to usurp the place of the former, and whether it is not now urgently called to repent of its unbelief?

NOTES

1   Beginning at Proverbs 22.17 and continuing into the next chapter.
2   The translation is that of the Revised Version, which is regularly used in this essay because of its literal character, though sometimes with slight emendation.
3   For a general survey of the wisdom literature, see Harry Ranston, *The Old Testament Wisdom Books and their Teaching* (London 1930). A brief survey of more recent discussion may be found in R. K. Harrison, *Introduction to the Old Testament* (London 1970), pp. 1004–9.
4   It is generally recognized today that apocalyptic has links with wisdom literature as well as with prophecy. Daniel was 'chief governor over all the wise men of Babylon', the words 'wise' and 'wisdom' occur in the book twenty-six times, and M. L. Margolis has argued that it was as being wisdom literature that Daniel was assigned to the Hagiographa of the Hebrew Bible, like Job, Proverbs and Ecclesiastes. For a discussion of this question, see ch. 4 of my book *The Old Testament Canon of the New Testament Church, and its Background in Early Judaism* (London 1986).
5   The moral implications of wisdom are also indicated (though without the use of the word) by the way the New Testament regularly links faith with repentance, by the statements about the knowledge of God in 1 John 2.4; 3.6; 4.8; and by expressions like 'obedience of faith' (Rom. 1.5; 16.26), 'obedience to the truth' (1 Pet. 1.22), 'obedient to the faith' (Acts 6.7), 'obey the teaching' (Rom. 6.17), 'obey the truth' (Rom. 2.8; Gal. 5.7), 'obey the gospel' (2 Thess. 1.8; 1 Pet. 4.17), 'obey the word' (1 Pet. 3.1), 'do the truth' (1 John 1.6). Attention has properly been drawn to the significance of these expressions by J. I. Packer.
6   In support of the rendering 'collections of sentences' (cf. RSV), see the commentaries of C. H. H. Wright and G. A. Barton (International

Critical Commentary), *ad loc*. The Revised Version has 'masters of assemblies'(cf. NEB).

7 For a possible reconstruction of the course of these events, see my article 'The Pre-History and Relationships of the Pharisees, Sadducees and Essenes', in *Revue de Qumran*, no. 41 (October 1982).

8 See also Mark 2.16; 7.1–23; Luke 18.12. The rules of the Pharisaic societies were to buy and eat only tithed foodstuffs, and to eat even common food in ceremonial cleanness (*Mishnah Demai*, 2.2f; *Tosephta Demai*, 2.2). The latter rule led to the insistence on washing of hands before meals, and both rules to caution about whom one ate with.

9 For a careful recent discussion of this saying, see I. H. Marshall, *The Gospel of Luke* (Exeter 1978), pp. 430–9.

10 The commentaries of 1 Corinthians chiefly consulted in preparing this part of the essay have been those of Robertson and Plummer (ICC), F. W. Grosheide (New International Commentary) and J. Héring (ET, London 1962).

11 See Eph. 1.9; 3.3f., 9; 5.32; Col. 1.26f. The term is also used in Rom. 16.25; 1 Cor. 4.1; 13.2; 14.2; Eph. 6.19; Col. 2.2; 4.3; 1 Tim. 3.9, but without explanation, except that it refers to the Gospel or some part of it. The only other places in the Pauline literature where it is used of specified truths are Rom. 11.25 and 1 Tim. 3.16.

12 For a discussion of the Greek background of the opening chapters of 1 Corinthians, and a somewhat different approach to the distinction between the 'babes' and the 'full-grown', see the Oxford D. Phil. thesis of Duane Litfin (unpublished).

13 *Philosophy and the Christian Faith* (London 1969), p. 47.

14 See John Rogerson, *Old Testament Criticism in the Nineteeth Century* (London 1984), p. 17. This is from Rogerson's introductory chapter on the eighteenth century, which is inevitably rather sketchy, but his point is undoubtedly true. What may be reckoned the complementary work to Rogerson's, H. Graf von Reventlow, *The Authority of the Bible and the Rise of the Modern World* (ET, London 1984), stops short in the early years of that century and only hints at what is to follow.

15 H. Graf von Reventlow, op. cit., in note 14, p. 412, etc. According to von Reventlow, the antecedents of this humanistic thinking went back to the Middle Ages. It had hitherto existed alongside the biblicism of the Reformers, which it now started to replace.

16 On the other hand, there have been serious attempts made, both by Anglo-Catholics such as Pusey and by confessional Protestants such as Hengstenberg, to utilize the new learning in illustrating and defending the Bible and not in undermining it. On Hengstenberg, see Rogerson, ch. 5. On Pusey, see the previous essay and Andrew Louth, 'The Oxford Movement, the Fathers and the Bible' in *Sobornost* 6.1 (1984).

PART TWO

Recovering the Authority of God

3 The Desecularization of Science

PETER HODGSON

Science now appears to be almost completely secular. The day-to-day life of the scientist, his mode of work, his choice of research problems, his assessment of his results and his relations with his colleagues are almost entirely independent of his religious beliefs. It is quite possible for scientists to work together for years without learning what they each individually believe concerning the most fundamental questions of human existence. Thus it would seem that science as it is today, as a body of knowledge and a way of life, is completely distinct from religion. If science and religion are discussed together it is only to contrast their different methods and points of view; science dealing with the detailed understanding of the world and religion with fundamental questions concerning the purpose of human life. If they interact at all it is because science in its onward march now and then encounters obstacles raised by religion, as when some form of experimentation is called immoral.

And yet, despite all this, there is now a growing realization that there are deeper connections between science and religion that cannot be ignored. Science on its own may appear to be secular, but it is embedded in a religious matrix from which it derives its very being and its ultimate justification, and furthermore as it grows and develops it raises insistent questions that can only be answered within that larger religious context.

It is now increasingly recognized that science presupposes very special beliefs about the material world, and that these are specifically Christian beliefs. Within this perspective it is possible to understand why science was born and came to maturity in our European Christian civilization and not in any of the great civilizations of antiquity. These presuppositions of science are so evident to us that we take them for granted without question. Yet ultimately science depends on them, so if it is transplanted to a society that does not hold them, it will have the greatest difficulty in taking root. Furthermore, if a society repudiates the Christian roots of science it is to be expected that its science will languish and die.

As science develops it raises a whole series of philosophical questions more or less related to religious beliefs. Studies of the atomic or nuclear world raise questions about space and time, chance and causality. The philosophical implications of quantum mechanics are actively debated, and it is becoming clearer that positivism is inadequate and that some form of realism is to be preferred. Studies of the evolution of the universe now raise questions concerning its origin and its purpose that cannot be answered from within science.

These questions concerning the relation of science to religion will be discussed in more detail in the following pages.

MECHANISM AND THE MISUNDERSTANDING OF 'SCIENCE'

The continuing advance of science affects every aspect of our lives, from the ideas and concepts that form the substance of our thoughts to the machines and products that we use every day. It is particularly in the realm of ideas and concepts that the advance of science influences our theological thinking, and this in turn affects the secularization of our culture.

Modern science owes its birth to Newton, who first showed how to steer the middle course between the empiricism of Bacon and the rationalism of Descartes. Using and developing the concepts of space and time, mass and force, velocity and acceleration, momentum and energy that had been gradually refined over the preceding centuries he formulated his laws of motion and showed how they could be used to calculate both celestial and terrestrial motions, the orbit of the moon and the fall of an apple. At the same time he developed the differential calculus and showed how this powerful mathematical technique can be used to express his laws of motion in concise and elegant form. The equations can be solved to find out very precisely how matter behaves in various circumstances. He thus laid the foundations of theoretical physics, and the extraordinary growth of science since his time has been essentially a development and extension to other realms of phenomena of the method first due to him.

So rapid was this development that by the nineteenth century it was possible to give a detailed account of practically all the evident phenomena of the physical world: the motions of the solar system; the phenomena of optics; heat, light and sound; magnetism and electricity. Indeed it seemed to the confident Victorians that the whole world of physical phenomena could be understood as a vast mechanism obeying Newton's laws.

This intellectual achievement exerted a wide influence on other areas of human activity. The Newtonian method was seen as the ideal road to knowledge and many attempts were made, with meagre success, to apply it outside the area of the physical sciences. The contrast between the objectivity and precision of science and the apparently irreconcilable discord in philosophical and theological circles made a deep impression. Here at last, it seemed, was a reliable road to the truth, and all else must be judged against its standards. The world *is* a vast mechanism and everything, including the activities of man, must be understood on that basis. Theology was not excepted from this: if the Bible records any events that appear to contradict Newton's laws, then so much the worse for the Bible. In this way science becomes an exegetical touchstone.

It will of course be noticed that all this goes far beyond what is actually required by the scientific discoveries themselves. Because certain phenomena now obey certain laws, we have no reason to say that certain other phenomena, said to have happened in the past, could not have taken place. It is not necessary, and indeed it is dangerous, to adopt a general Humean scepticism to show this. It is sufficient to remark that there may be forces of some kind acting in one situation and not in the other. Since the material world owes its very being to God, it is entirely within God's power to override the operation of those laws that normally determine its behaviour.

This is a particular instance of a very general phenomenon of the highest importance for the present discussion: it is not the strict results of scientific inquiry that have the greatest influence on our beliefs but rather the popular interpretation and extrapolation of scientific achievements. Thus scientists find that some aspects of the world show mechanical behaviour, therefore the world is no more than a vast mechanism, and therefore nothing that is inconsistent with that mechanism is credible. All this is of course quite unjustified, with no logical force. But it has immense psychological force, and has moulded the thoughts of generations.

It is quite consistent with this interpretation that the grip of mechanism was released not by philosophical arguments but by the development of a new physics that was no longer mechanical. This in its turn has been largely misunderstood and taken to have implications that do not survive careful analysis. This theme of the collapse of mechanism and the rise of the new physics will be considered in more detail later on, but before doing so it is desirable to clarify the relation between theology and science.

THEOLOGY AND SCIENCE

At first sight theology and science would appear to be quite distinct activities, the one concerned with understanding God and the other with understanding the world. Such a sharp separation is not acceptable because we believe that God created the world and we must ask how that affects the practice and indeed the very existence of science. Furthermore, some interpretations of scientific discoveries appear to lend support to some theological beliefs, while others apparently do the opposite. Our knowledge is, or should be, an indivisible whole, and so we must face the question of the relation of theology to science. Which of these forms of knowledge is prior? If theology, then how can we safeguard the integrity of science, and if science, then how can we preserve our most fundamental beliefs? How, and according to what criteria, are any differences to be settled?

This is enough to show that the relation of theology to science is by no means simple. Many of the difficulties stem however from thinking of theology and science as two existing bodies of knowledge that have somehow to be related. It is now being increasingly recognized that this is not a fruitful way to tackle the question, and that the proper way to do this is to examine the historical development of science, and in particular the reasons why it appeared in history at the time and place it did. The origin of science thus provides the key to the understanding of the relation of theology to science.

It has been mentioned already that modern science was born at a particular place and time in human history, namely in Europe in the seventeenth century. Why did this happen? Why did science not develop in any of the great civilizations of antiquity? We easily forget that science is a very special, relatively recent and indeed unique occurrence in human history. During the last three millennia there have been a dozen or so great civilizations, with highly organized cities, most notable artistic achievements, well-developed political systems, great literature and drama, sophisticated philosophy, impressive architecture and art, and yet nothing that we would really call science.

We find highly-developed technical skills in the working of wood and metal, stone and ceramics, but not a detailed understanding of the behaviour of matter, expressed in mathematical terms. There is often a well-organized system of land measurement and a knowledge of the apparent motions of the stars and the planets, but no understanding of the way these motions can be calculated by solving the equations of dynamics. There may be speculations about the ultimate constituents of matter, but no definite idea of their size and structure, or theory of their properties and the relation of these properties to those of everyday matter. Above all, there is no conception of the way all the infinite variety of phenomena, astronomical, electrical, dynamical, chemical and atomic, can be understood as the manifestations of a simple essential unity that can be expressed by a few differential equations.

WHY SCIENCE DEVELOPS

Viewed in the context of the whole of human history the development of science is an extraordinary occurrence that makes our civilization quite unlike any other. To understand why and how this happened is a complicated historical question that can be approached by studying the conditions that are necessary for the birth of science, and then seeing to what extent these conditions are present in the different civilizations. If we find that these conditions are present only in Europe in the seventeenth century, then we have as full an explanation as it is possible to have for a historical phenomenon.

There are several conditions that must evidently be satisfied for science to develop. The society must be so organized that it is possible for some of its members to have sufficient leisure to think about the world. It needs the materials and tools to make apparatus for experiments, a system of writing and some mathematics. These are the material necessities of science, but since they are found in most of the civilisations of antiquity we must look elsewhere for the reasons for the unique birth of science.

Is it not possible that whether science develops or not depends on the attitude of the people to the material world? Some attitudes might actually prevent anyone thinking about the world in a way likely to lead to science, while others might at least provide a fertile soil for its growth. What beliefs about the world might be expected to do this? First of all, there must be some conviction that the world is in some sense good, and that it is worthwhile and respectable to try to find out something about it. Another essential belief is that matter is orderly, that it behaves in a rational and consistent way. Unless we believe that there is an order in nature we will never take the trouble to find out what it is. This order might be a necessary order, so that the world cannot be made in any way except the way it is in fact made. If we believed this, then we might try to find out about it by pure thought, without making experiments. Some people have indeed tried this, but they have not got very far. We know that the only way to find out about the world is by controlled observation and experiment, and this is not encouraged if we believe that the order of the world is a necessary order. The other possibility is that this world is only one among many possibilities. That is, we could believe that the order of the world is contingent, that it could be other than it is. If we believe this, then the only way to ascertain that order is by observation and experiment, and thus the way is open for the development of science.

Another requirement for the development of science is the belief that the whole enterprise is a practicable one. The order in nature must to some extent be open to the human mind, so that we can discover it. There also needs to be some strong motivation to carry the scientist through the inevitable difficulties and disappointments. Finally, science is a co-operative endeavour, the work of many minds, so it is also necessary to believe that whatever knowledge he gains is not his alone, but must be shared with the whole community.

These are the main beliefs that must be held before science can even begin. They need not be held consciously or explicitly; indeed to us they are so obvious that we would hardly think of formulating them. They are part of the very fabric of our thought and form the way we look at the world. Yet in spite of this, they constitute a very special set of beliefs that is by no means universal in human history. In fact if we examine the beliefs of the civilizations of antiquity we do not find them, and this is the explanation why science did not develop in them.[1]

The very special set of beliefs about the material world that is needed for the growth of science did exist in Europe in the seventeenth century, and this is why science as we know it developed at that time. But what was the origin of those beliefs, and why were they present at that time?

THE CHRISTIAN ORIGINS OF MODERN SCIENCE

In the seventeenth century, and for several centuries before then, the thought of Europe had been moulded by Christian theology. Everyone, from the peasant to the king, thought of the world in Christian terms. We must therefore examine how the beliefs that we have seen are necessary for the development of science are related to Christian beliefs about the world. We will find in every case that there is a very close relation between the two sets of beliefs, so that it was the Christian creed that prepared the way for science by teaching men just that particular attitude to the material world that is necessary for the growth of science.

We can see this in detail by going through the beliefs already mentioned. The Christian believes that the world is good because God made it so: 'And God saw all he had made, and indeed it was very good' (Gen. 1.31). Matter was further ennobled by the incarnation: 'The Word was made flesh and he lived amongst us' (John 1.14). The world is rational and orderly because it was made and is kept in being by a rational God. It is contingent because it depends on the divine fiat: God could have chosen to make the world in a different way. There is here a delicate balance between the freedom and the rationality of God: tip the balance one way or the other and you have a belief in a chaotic or a necessary world, both inimical to the growth of science. Finally the Christian believes that the world can be apprehended by the human mind because God commanded man to subdue the earth, and he does not command the impossible. Thus the Christian mind is steeped through and through with the attitude to the material world that is necessary for the development of science.

The Christian also has the strongest motivation to study the world. Christ himself reiterates the divine command to subdue the earth when by the Parable of the Talents he urges us to make full use of all our faculties and powers. Furthermore, as soon as it becomes clear that scientific knowledge can be applied to grow more food and improve his medical care, to provide better clothes and housing, it becomes a special obligation on man to do this in view of the injunction

117

to feed the hungry, to give drink to the thirsty and to clothe the naked.

The remaining condition for the development of science, the belief that knowledge must be freely shared, is enjoined by the Book of Wisdom: 'What I have learned without self-interest, I pass on without reserve: I do not intend to hide her riches. For she is an inexhaustible treasure to men, and those who acquire it win God's friendship' (Wisd. 7.13).

We thus find that during the critical centuries before the birth of science the collective mind of Europe was moulded by a system of beliefs that included just those special elements that are necessary for the birth and growth of science. There is thus a living organic continuity between the Christian revelation and modern science; Christianity provided just those beliefs that are essential for science, and the moral climate that encouraged its growth. As Whitehead has remarked, 'the faith in the possibility of science, generated antecedently to the development of modern scientific theory, is an unconscious derivative from medieval theology'.[2] In many cases indeed it was by no means unconscious: the pioneers of modern science often saw themselves as revealing the works of God, and theological arguments feature explicitly in the development of their ideas.

This brief sketch of the vital contribution of the Christian faith to the rise of modern science raises many historical questions that cannot be followed in detail here. How, for example, did the ancient Greeks manage to make such a brilliant start, and yet ultimately their science was still-born? Why did science take seventeen hundred years after the birth of Christ to get going? Does science manage to flourish in non-Christian and even in anti-Christian societies?

The failure of Greek science was partly a consequence of the very fertility and multiplicity of ideas at that time. Some outstanding individuals such as Archimedes had many of the right ideas, but they lived in a society influenced by many other ideas inimical to science. So although an important start was made by a few thinkers, they lacked the massive support of the whole community. In the later centuries the initial impetus was lost, a profound pessimism permeated Greek society, and Greek science faded into oblivion.

In the first centuries of the Christian era the persecuted and scattered believers lived in the expectation of the imminent second coming of Christ, and any interest in the workings of the material world seemed to them a vain curiosity. Yet implicit in the gospel are new ideas about the relation of God, man and nature that gradually over the centuries prepared the mind of Europe for the first viable birth of science. After the fall of the Roman Empire, Christianity kept alive the learning of the ancient world together with a faith in the purpose and rationality of human existence. Gradually a new world came into being, a world largely moulded by the Christian faith, and in the Christian society of the Middle Ages the ideas brought into the world so many centuries earlier developed and flowered. In the early Middle Ages the works of classical antiquity, particularly those of Aristotle, became known in the Christian West, and soon came to exert a strong influence on Christian thought. Aristotle asked many of the right questions about nature, but they could not be answered within his constricting set of ideas. The means of breaking out of this system was provided by the ideas implicit in the Christian faith and it was this fusion of Greek questions and the Christian faith that led in a few centuries to the birth of science.

The Christian philosophers and theologians of the Middle Ages welded their knowledge into a coherent whole using the current ideas of the material world, mainly derived from Aristotle. When these ideas of the world were radically changed by the development of modern science it was difficult for the Christians of the time to see that this in no way threatened their Christian beliefs. This misunderstanding was complicated by the religious upheavals of the times, and these tended to harden attitudes and to prevent the careful and objective analysis required by the new situation. Much of this misunderstanding persists to the present day, and is reinforced by the actions of many Christians who do not know that science has its roots in Christianity. It is worth recalling that most of the scientists responsible for the early development of science were themselves convinced Christians who saw their scientific work as an essential part of their Christian vocation.

A more urgent and contemporary question is the relation of science and theology today. It could well be argued that however science managed to get going in the past, that is of no interest to us now. Once launched, science has shown such intrinsic vitality that it is now entirely independent of its theological roots. Indeed, does science not flourish exceedingly in atheistic societies such as Soviet Russia?

119

Peter Hodgson

SOVIET SCIENCE

It is generally considered that science in the Soviet Union is of high quality, and certainly no efforts are spared by the Soviet media to praise its achievements. It would seem that science flourishes in the Soviet Union, and this is indeed what might be expected, since Marxism-Leninism claims to be essentially a scientific view of the world. If all this is true, then it would seriously weaken the alleged connection between Christian theology and science.

Marx claimed to have discovered a basic set of rules that are valid in both the natural and the social sciences.[3] If this is so, then science has at last found its natural home, and should flourish as never before. But if it is false, then, since Marxism has political power, the stage is set for the enslavement of science. Engels told the scientists that they would no longer be able to do as they pleased: 'Whatever pose natural scientists adopt, philosophy rules over them. The question is only whether they want to be ruled by some vile fashionable philosophy, or whether they want to be guided by a form of theoretical thought that is grounded on acquaintance with the history of thought and its achievements.'[4]

Lenin was aware of the revolution in physics during the early years of this century, and connected this with his political revolution: 'Modern physics is in travail: it is giving birth to dialectical materialism.'[5]

In the early years of the revolution attention was concentrated on the economic difficulties and internal struggles, but by 1931 Stalin was able to turn his attention to science. Bukharin threatened scientists with 'physical and moral guillotine',[6] meaning the systematic imposition of Marxism. Throughout the 1930s, scientists were forced to subscribe to Marxist doctrine, and many who resisted were purged from the Academy. In a speech in 1947 Zhdanov called for a fight against 'countless philosophical weeds' and even against 'smuggling God into science'.[7] Einstein's theory of relativity was condemned, and the theory of molecular bonding suffered the same fate. Genetics was destroyed by Lysenko, and Vavilov, the greatest of the Russian geneticists, was exiled to his death in Siberia.

In 1952, I. V. Kuznetsov, a party theoretician, wrote on the relation of science to dialectical materialism, and claimed that 'Soviet physics is the standard-bearer for the most modern and progressive ideas of contemporary natural science'. Turning his attention to relativity, he declared that the development of science can only be secured by 'the total renunciation of Einstein's conception, without compromise or half-measure'.[8]

Physicists of the stature of Landau, who had hitherto kept out of the ideological dispute, rebelled against this nonsense. They could argue from a secure position of strength. Whatever the Marxist theoreticians say, the real world goes on behaving according to its intrinsic nature. You may rewrite history to your heart's content, and if you control the media and the educational system, no one will stop you. But if you insist on designing a nuclear accelerator without using Einstein's equations, then on the great day when you switch it on for the first time, nothing will happen. Considerations such as this convinced the party theoreticians that science, and particularly physics, must be accorded some measure of autonomy. It must, however, still be subjected to the demands of dialectical materialism.

Soviet science then moved into a new phase. The scientists must be allowed to carry on their work according to scientific criteria, but the aims of the research must be governed by the needs of society. The main strength of State direction appears when there is a well-defined objective, such as to make an atomic bomb, or to launch a satellite. Even these achievements, it may be noted, relied greatly on Western science, the one on the international work at Los Alamos, and the other on the German research at Pennemunde, which was taken over by the Red Army at the end of the war.

In other areas the results of State direction are less impressive. The Soviet accelerator at Dubna, like most Soviet instruments, was designed to be the biggest in the world. It was certainly one of the heaviest, with 30,000 tons of steel, but it was heavily and clumsily engineered, and never fulfilled its high hopes. Soviet computers are slow and inefficient by Western standards, and the Soviet copy of Concorde was a monumental failure.

So great is the intrinsic vitality of science, that excellent work continues to be done, even under severe disadvantages. Landau was certainly one of the greatest theoretical physicists of the century, and Tamm, Migdal, Čerenkov, Kurchatov, Fock, Bogliubov, Kapitza, Markov and Sakharov are names that will always be remembered by physicists. Most of them, however, suffered difficulties at one time or another, and in particular the treatment of Sakharov is well known.

121

Many other scientists have suffered a similar or a worse fate, being sent to forced labour camps or denied the right to emigrate.

It is, however, important to place in their proper perspective particular incidents and statements by particular individuals. There is no great political or religious movement without its scandals due to the ignorance and stupidity of some of its followers. The history of science in Western Europe shows many instances of the persecution of scientists and the inept handling of scientific matters, and it is easy but misleading to make a catalogue of such incidents. The important issue is whether they are accidental events attributable to human weakness, or whether they are the result of the inexorable working-out of the fundamental principles of the movement under examination.

It is thus important to assess, in an objective way, the world-standing of pure science in the Soviet Union. Is it what would be expected of a superpower, comparable with the United States of America in so many other respects? In an attempt to answer this question, John Baker in 1945 compiled in an objective way some of the most important scientific discoveries made during the two world wars.[9] It was then found that this work was mainly done in the United States, Germany and Britain. None of it was done in the Soviet Union. More recently, several studies have been made of the contributions to conferences and to the main scientific journals. These figures led to the inescapable conclusion that the quantity of first-rate science coming from the Soviet Union is among the lowest per capita of all the countries with substantial research programmes. In absolute quantity, it is comparable with that from a medium-sized European country.

This is the objective measure of the state of science in one of the great superpowers of the world, a country that exalts science, that has numerous huge universities where scientific studies have high priority, that honours its scientific Academicians with lavish favours, that founds science cities, that pours out ceaseless propaganda praising the supreme excellence of its scientific achievements, that pours scorn on the decadent science of the West, that claims to found its ideology on scientific principles and to be the one nation able to lead mankind to a glorious and scientific heaven on earth.

We would expect, would we not, that science, having struggled into being, God knows how, in the intellectual morass of religion-ridden Europe, would, when transplanted into the pure soil of Marxism-

Leninism, flourish and grow to the wonder and astonishment of the world.

The facts, however, are otherwise. Could it be that another interpretation should be considered? That science, born and nourished in Christian Europe, including, as time went on, Christian Russia, found itself after the Revolution in alien soil, a soil repugnant to its nature and inimical to its growth. But so great is the natural vitality of science, so strong the genius of the Russian people, that even in this alien soil science manages to survive, and now and then to produce brilliant results. The heavy hand of State direction, the lack of intellectual freedom, the ideological oppression, the censorship, the prevention of travel and communication, is enough to cow and crush all but the bravest spirits, so that Soviet science, taken as a whole, falls far short of what would be expected from a great country.

QUANTUM PHYSICS

In the nineteenth century the edifice of classical physics seemed almost complete. The material world could be explained as a vast mechanism, and its motions calculated from Newton's laws. It seemed to the scientists of the time that there was little more to do but to measure a few more phenomena to an extra decimal place.

And yet this confidence in the finality of physics was entirely mistaken. Within a few years came Planck's discovery that energy is always transferred in finite amounts called quanta, Einstein's theory of relativity and the quantum mechanics of Born, Schrödinger, Heisenberg and Dirac. A wealth of atomic and nuclear phenomena was discovered, and explained in great detail by the new quantum mechanics. Taken together, it was one of the most profound and far-reaching achievements of the human mind.

The implications of this new way of understanding the world are still actively debated. The old Victorian mechanism is gone for ever, but what has taken its place is far from clear. Physicists are accustomed to use quantum mechanics in the course of their work, but seldom give much thought to its wider meaning. Several of the pioneers of modern physics held strong views on the subject, and wrote books describing the strange phenomena of the quantum world. Frequently they claimed that quantum physics has profound philosophical implications such as the destruction of causality and determinism, the abolition of

123

the distinction between the observer and the observed, the wave-particle duality of matter and the unified nature of the universe. These in turn have often been held to have theological implications as well: the collapse of mechanism has been thought to open the door to miracles and free-will while indeterminism seems to undercut traditional arguments for the existence of God.[10]

To find out what truth there is in all this it is essential to look closely at what has actually been found experimentally, and to distinguish it carefully from preconceived philosophical standpoints. We then find that what are frequently advertised as the philosophical or even theological implications of modern physics are nearly always attributable to the philosophical presuppositions of the scientist, and not to his actual results. Frequently these presuppositions are more implicit than explicit, and often they are contrary to those on which science itself is based.

Physicists, whether they realize it or not, are strongly affected by the prevailing philosophical climate, and so if we are to understand the implications of modern physics it is necessary to begin by describing the views that were prevalent around the turn of the century. At the time many physicists, particularly on the Continent, were strongly influenced by Mach's sensationalism. Partly as a reaction against the exhuberant mechanism of the nineteenth century, and partly because of the economy of thought it undoubtedly brings, they admitted to science only those quantities that are directly apprehended by the senses. Within this perspective science is reduced to the most convenient and economical arrangement of our sense impressions, and all reference to an underlying reality is excluded. This led Mach to deny the reality of atoms, a denial only shaken when he was shown the scintillations on a zinc sulphide screen due to alpha-particles (helium nuclei) from a radioactive source. In the following decades, Mach's theory of science was further developed by the well-known Vienna Circle of positivist philosophers of science.

Quantum theory, and later on quantum mechanics, was developed in this philosophical climate, and a comprehensive philosophical interpretation of quantum mechanics was developed in Copenhagen by Niels Bohr, one of the principal architects of the quantum theory of atomic structure. According to this interpretation, physics is essentially concerned with the relations between measurable observables. The values of all observable quantities may be calculated from the wavefunction of the system, which contains all the information concerning that system.

This interpretation was generally shared and developed further by Heisenberg particularly in connection with his uncertainty principle. This he interpreted as an insurmountable barrier between the observer and reality, so that physics had reached the end of the road.[11] Since it was therefore impossible to reach the ultimate reality, it meant for him that 'objective reality has evaporated'.[12]

Bohr also accepted quantum mechanics as the end of the road. He did this, in the words of Popper, 'partly in despair: only classical physics was understandable, was a description of reality. Quantum mechanics was not a description of reality. Such a description was impossible to achieve in the atomic region: apparently because no such reality existed: the understandable reality ended where classical physics ended.'[13]

Initially, Einstein was strongly influenced by Mach, but later on his scientific creativity forced him to repudiate sensationalism and to affirm that 'the belief in an external world independent of the perceiving subject is the basis of all natural science'.[14] In his autobiography he remarks: 'In my younger years, Mach's epistemological position influenced me very greatly, a position which today appears to me to be essentially untenable'.[15] Einstein argued that since quantum mechanics does not provide, even in principle, answers to many physically reasonable questions, it must be incomplete. It is an essentially statistical theory and gives the average behaviour of a large number or ensemble of systems, but an incomplete account of the behaviour of each individual system. Thus essentially nothing has changed since Galileo, or Newton, or Faraday concerning the status or role of the 'observer' or of our 'consciousness' or of our 'information' in physics.[16]

Einstein's repudiation of the Copenhagen interpretation was shared by several other physicists, including Planck, Schrödinger, von Laue and de Broglie, but the majority of physicists preferred to follow Bohr, and even today his views generally prevail.

Einstein never regarded his own great advances as anything but single steps on a long road. To the end of his life he strove to improve on what he had already done. Bohr and Heisenberg, on the other hand, believed that quantum mechanics is the final theory, so that nothing more remains to be said about the fundamental nature of the material world.

Quite apart from the general arguments against this position, the actual development of nuclear physics soon showed that the quantum-mechanical description of reality is incomplete. Thus in the 1930s it was found that the nucleus is made up of smaller particles called protons and neutrons, and positive electrons were discovered. In the following years many short-lived unstable particles were also found, and the protons and neutrons were themselves found to be made up of even smaller particles called quarks. If physicists had seriously believed the Copenhagen interpretation they would never have embarked on the researches that led to these discoveries.

In every age there is a marked tendency to consider the existing theoretical structure of physics as the final one, so that there remains little to do but to tidy up a few corners and to increase the accuracy of some measurements. Always such views have been made ridiculous by the further development of science. There is no reason to believe our present knowledge to be an exception. This consideration should make us very cautious about drawing any far-reaching conclusions from the present state of science.

The central issue in what Popper has called the schism in physics is that between realism and idealism. On the one hand Einstein affirms the existence of a real world independent of any human observer, that existed before us, exists now and will exist long after the last man has perished. Bohr, on the other hand, considered our subjective impressions to be more real than the world, which is indeed no more than a construction of our own minds.

Quantum mechanics can be presented as a formal axiomatic theory which specifies how to calculate any experimentally observable quantity. It does, however, leave unanswered many questions that it is still very natural to ask. The vital point here is whether quantum mechanics is a complete theory, or whether it is a partial or statistical theory. If it is a complete theory, then any questions that it cannot answer must be dismissed as meaningless, and it is a waste of time to try to answer them. If it is not a complete theory, then it is important to see if we can find a way of answering such questions.

The completeness of quantum mechanics has implications for the concept of causality, and hence for one of the traditional ways to God. In the Second Way of St Thomas, God is identified as the first cause. This argument depends on the belief that every material event is efficiently caused, that there are prior events that make it what it is.

This priority has been taken by some commentators to be a temporal priority, and furthermore it has been claimed that modern physics has found events with no material antecedents whatsoever. This had led Heisenberg to say that 'the invalidity of the law of causality is definitely proved by quantum mechanics'. If all this is correct, then it would appear that the Second Way had been invalidated by modern physics.

However, it must first be pointed out that in the Second Way St Thomas was not concerned to argue for God as something which, by acting in the past, is responsible for current phenomena. In his view, God is outside time, so that even if one has a causal sequence infinitely extended in time then the whole sequence still depends on the sustaining power of God to keep it in existence. Thus even if there are events without temporal antecedents they would still require God's causality to account for their being. Secondly, that argument that some nuclear phenomena have no temporal antecedents depends on the belief that quantum mechanics provides a complete description of reality, which as we have seen is a philosophical belief that cannot be established by science. If this belief is not accepted, then we can easily imagine that there are causal antecedents that have not yet been found.

This may be illustrated by the phenomenon of radioactive decay. Many nuclei and particles are unstable; after a certain time they decay in a characteristic way. There is no known way of predicting the instant of decay of a particular nucleus or particle. We can, however, establish in each case a half-life, which gives the probability of decay in each instant of time. This half-life can be measured by observing a large number of decays, and in many cases it can be understood in terms of the structure of the nucleus or the theory of elementary particles. The behaviour of a large number of nuclei or particles is thus determined and calculable.

But can any cause be assigned to the instant of decay of a particular nucleus? According to the Copenhagen interpretation of quantum mechanics, all nuclei of the same type are identical, and all possible information that can be obtained from measurements on any one of them is contained in the wavefunction and this gives only the probability of decay per unit time.

The answer to this question is determined by philosophical and not scientific considerations, although it does inevitably have scientific implications. If we believe that the only admissible statements about

127

the world are those that can be verified by a definite sequence of operations and measurements in the laboratory, then questions about the cause of a particular radioactive decay at a particular instant of time must be dismissed as without meaning. On the other hand, if we believe that the thinking of the scientist should not always be constrained by the theoretical framework existing at the present time then we will want to persist in asking such questions and in trying to find answers to them.

FROM POSITIVISM TO REALISM

It is worth remarking at this point that scientists very frequently introduce into their work ideas and concepts that cannot be measured. This has been defended by J. J. Thomson: 'I hold that if the introduction of a quantity promotes clearness of thought, then even if at the moment we have no means of determining it with precision, its introduction is not only legitimate but desirable. The immeasurable of today may be the measurable of tomorrow. It is dangerous to base a philosophy on the assumption that what I know not can never be knowledge'.[17]

It is indeed evident that there is a considerable jump between the statements 'I do not know of a cause of the decay of this nucleus at this instant of time' and 'there is no cause for this decay'. One can without difficulty postulate a number of possible causes. For example, although all nuclei of a particular type appear to be the same, we know that they are composed of a large number of particles (neutrons and protons) in constant motion, and it is easy to suppose that the motions are different in each individual nucleus, and that the decay occurs when the appropriate configuration is reached. If we knew these motions, and the 'hidden variables' describing them, we could in principle predict the instant of decay. Another possibility is that the decay is triggered by some external influence such as a particle that cannot easily be detected.

Experimentally, this is still an open question, but there has been much discussion of the possibility that the presence of such hidden variables can be excluded on quite general theoretical grounds. As early as 1932 von Neumann devised a proof that no such hidden variables are possible in quantum mechanics.[18] Subsequently, however, it was realized that his proof is based on unnecessarily restrictive assumptions, and if these are removed the proof no longer holds. There has been extensive discussion of these arguments since then.[19] It may be doubted whether such general arguments can ever tell us about such a fundamental feature of the world. As John Polkinghorne has recently reminded us, 'if the study of science teaches one anything, it is that it is unwise to try to lay down beforehand by pure thought what will actually prove to be the case. Reality is often so much more subtle than we imagine'.[20] Quantum mechanics is certainly not a completely deterministic theory, but that does not imply that the same is the case for the underlying reality that it partially describes.

A further illustration of this is provided by Heisenberg's Uncertainty Principle, which is generally understood to say that the product of the uncertainties in the position and the momentum of a particle is always greater than Planck's constant. Similar relations hold for other pairs of variables such as energy and time. The more accurately we measure one of these variables, the less accurate is the result of our measurement of the other variable. This is sometimes taken to mean that particles do not have a definite position and momentum.

If, however, we go back to the basic physics we find rather a different situation. We can, for example, consider the diffraction of a beam of electrons by a slit. In this experiment, a collimated beam of electrons of the same energy is directed towards a narrow slit, and a screen is placed on the other side of the slit. As they pass through the slit the directions of motion of the electrons are changed so that they fan out over a certain angular range, just like diffraction in optics. It is found that the narrower the slit, the wider the angular range of the fan, as in the corresponding optical experiment.

If now we consider motion in a direction perpendicular to that of the incident electron beam, then the uncertainty in position is the width of the slit, and the uncertainty in transverse momentum is calculable from the mean angle of deviation of the electrons after they have emerged from the slit. If now we examine these two uncertainties, we find that they indeed satisfy Heisenberg's Uncertainty Principle.

It is, however, possible to measure the momentum of each individual electron much more precisely. If we place a particle-detector on the screen behind the slit we can determine the point of arrival of each electron, and hence we can calculate its transverse momentum with an accuracy much greater than that corresponding to the distribution as a whole. Thus while it remains true that we cannot predict the transverse momentum of the electron after it has passed through the slit, nevertheless subsequent measurements enable it to be determined to an accuracy much greater than that specified by the Uncertainty Principle.[21] Thus physics gives us no grounds for saying that the position and momentum of the particle are unknowable within the limits of the Uncertainty Principle, and still less that it does not have position and momentum. Indeed, it is all perfectly compatible with each electron moving along a definite trajectory determined by forces in the vicinity of the slit that we are as yet unable to calculate or measure.

This example shows very clearly the essentially statistical nature of quantum mechanics. The measurements of the passage through the apparatus of a large number of electrons give the diffraction pattern; this is a statistical scatter distribution that is calculable by a statistical theory. A similar situation is found in problems of practical importance, such as the emission of particles from a nuclear reaction. The direction of emission of any individual particle is of no interest; what is important is the probability of emission as a function of angle. This is a statistical quantity, and its measured value is compared with the probability distribution calculated from the theory of the reaction.

If this interpretation is accepted, then the celebrated wave-particle duality is simply a category confusion. On the one hand we have particles moving along definite trajectories with definite momenta, and on the other we recognize that due to their interactions with the apparatus these trajectories have a certain probability distribution calculable from Schrödinger's equation. The so-called wave nature of these particles is no more an intrinsic property than, for example, actuarial statements are intrinsic properties of a particular individual.

There have been many discussions of the implications of quantum physics that implicitly accept the indeterminism of the Copenhagen interpretation. Thus William Pollard in his book *Chance and Providence* considers the problem of understanding the providential action of God in a world governed by deterministic physical laws, and finds a way out by invoking quantum indeterminacy. He accepts that physics 'has become statistical in its innermost core' so that 'no forces, external or internal, known or unknown, can eliminate the element of choice from the picture'. Thus 'at every moment the countless myriad of diverse elements which go to make up and define the state of the universe at that instant have each their separate choices to make among the alternative paths open to them'.

Within the perspective of the Christian revelation, this is not meaningless chaos but the action of God's providence: 'The Christian sees the chances and accidents of history as the very warp and woof of the fabric of providence which God is ever weaving. Seen in this way, they can be gladly and joyously acknowledged and accepted. But apart from this revelation, chance and accident mean anarchy, sheer meaningless random incoherence, and utter chaos from which the soul recoils in horror.'[22]

This interpretation implies that God shapes the course of history by continually guiding atomic events within the limits of the Heisenberg Uncertainty relations and subject to the overall probability distributions required by quantum mechanics. Whether such a conception of God's activity is satisfactory it is for the theologians to consider, but it is being argued here that there is an alternative possibility fully consistent with the results of modern science, namely that the material inanimate universe is a fully determined system evolving along a unique path in which each event is completely determined by its antecedents.

This does not, however, imply that the universe is a mechanical system; that possibility has been banished for ever by modern physics. This severely limits the extent to which we can imagine what happens, for example, when a gamma ray produces an electron-positron pair. But if some aspects of physical reality are beyond our imagination, this does not imply that they are unknowable or undetermined; indeed we can often obtain accurate mathematical descriptions of them.

The foregoing account of quantum physics shows how strongly positivist ideas have influenced the philosophical interpretation of quantum mechanics. Scientists frequently adopt the Copenhagen interpretation when talking about quantum mechanics, but remain realists in the actual conduct of their research. This ambiguity can be damaging, and in recent years there have been many instances of the debilitating effects of the denial of reality. This is being increasingly recognized, and there is now a decided shift away from positivist views of science and towards a more realist interpretation.[23]

Positivism and secularism are closely allied, since both accept empirical data but reject metaphysical interpretations. The shift from positivism to realism is thus a process of de-secularization. This process is even more marked in cosmology, the science of the universe as a whole.

SCIENCE AND CREATION

As a final illustration of the contemporary interactions of theology and science, we can consider the most fundamental question of the creation of the universe.

We have all, at one time or another, gazed at the starry sky and asked ourselves how it all began. Such reflections can lead to awe and reverence, and following the Psalmist we can rejoice that the heavens show forth the glory of the Lord. But then we might be depressed by the apparent insignificance of man: we are mere specks in the vastness of space and time. We can reflect with Pascal that 'man is but a reed, the most feeble thing in nature. The entire universe need not arm itself to crush him; a vapour, a drop of water suffices to kill him.' But then we can reply, again with Pascal, that man 'is a thinking reed. If the universe were to crush him, man would still be nobler than that which killed him, because he knows that he dies and the advantages the universe has over him; of this the universe knows nothing.'[24] But then is life and man just the result of some chance aggregation of atoms in an obscure corner of the universe, or is it possible to say that the universe was made for man, that it is in some sense his home? But if this is so, we can ask with Margaret Knight: 'If life is the purpose of creation, what conceivably can be the point of the countless millions of lifeless worlds? Or the aeons of astronomical time before life existed? The Church has glanced uneasily to these questions but it has never answered them.'[25]

These questions about the creation of the universe and its purpose have exercised men's minds since the dawn of civilization, and many answers have been given in terms of creation stories, intertwined with myth and speculation, but not based on firm evidence. This situation has changed dramatically in the last few years: now for the first time in history the whole universe, spread out through space and time, is the object of scientific study. Our understanding of the early history of the universe has proceeded apace, and now for the first time we are able to give a reasonably detailed quantitative account of the development of the universe from a moment when it was concentrated into a very small volume until the present time. Through the eyes of science we can now see back through space and time to the dawn of our era, and quantitative knowledge has apparently taken the place of religious speculation.

This scientific work is of great intrinsic interest, and it acquires added importance through its relations with religion, and these are our primary concern here. In the first place we are forced to define more clearly what we actually mean by creation, and whether the early history of the universe as revealed by the scientist has anything to do with the creation of the universe by God. Secondly, the developing scientific ideas have frequently impinged on the contemporary religious syntheses, leading to much confusion and conflict. And finally the development of the way we think about the universe, which forms the backdrop to our lives, inevitably influences in many subtle ways how we think about ourselves and our world.

In the simplest sense, creation means to produce or to bring into being, as for instance an artist creates a picture or a composer a symphony. These examples refer to the ordering of pre-existing materials or concepts into new meaningful relationships by the mind of man. The author of the first chapter of Genesis had in mind something much more fundamental than this, namely the Creation of the universe, of all that is, out of nothing by the power of God. This is a concept that we can know only by analogy with creation from pre-existing materials, and to distinguish it we give it a capital C.

The difficulties of the concept of Creation appear when we ask how we could possibly, even in principle, ever establish that the universe was once Created. We can imagine what it would mean for a particular object to be created out of nothing now, and we could observe it scientifically: at one instant we would observe nothing in a particular volume and at the next instant the object Created. This cannot, however, be done for the universe as a whole. Before the Creation there can be no observer except God himself, and no time or space in which Creation can take place, since time and space are Created together with the universe. Thus Creation is an event completely beyond the reach of man's observation. It is not an event that could, even in principle, be a proper subject for scientific discourse. No scientific result could ever establish that Creation took place, or that it did not take place. The 'age of the universe' is therefore not a scientific concept.

This is not to say that scientific studies of the universe are completely irrelevant to the Christian belief in Creation, for it is possible that the structure of the universe as revealed by science is most readily intelligible within a Christian theological context. Throughout history man has always sought a coherent and unified account of the world he lives in and the purpose of his life. It may well be that there are certain types of knowledge that he can attain by scientific investigation, and other types by philosophical reflection or by divine revelation, and that these different types of knowledge are not connected by deductive inference. That is, it is not possible to deduce his science from his theology or his theology from his science. There may nevertheless be other links between them that bind them into a coherent whole without affecting the intrinsic integrity of either way of knowledge. Thus it can be argued that the Christian beliefs concerning the nature of the material world provide the essential presuppositions underlying the whole scientific enterprise. The knowledge obtained from science, in its turn, is essential for the life of man, and shows forth in an ever more impressive way the goodness and power of the Creator.

The belief in Creation, so succinctly stated in Genesis, carries a wealth of meaning that sharply distinguishes the Judeo-Christian revelation from all other religions and determines, in the most radical way, the believer's outlook on life. It implies that God the Creator is completely distinct from his Creation, and that every particle and process in the universe is completely and continually dependent on his creative power. Creation is not a once-and-for-all activity by which God makes the universe and then lets it go on by itself; on the contrary, God's creative power is continually active in keeping it in being, and if it ceased for an instant the universe would lapse into nothingness. The universe does not depend on God as the picture on the painter, but as the song on the singer.

The Judeo-Christian belief in Creation absolutely excludes any identification between God and the universe such as is found in pantheism, and the Christian God is not the absentee God of deism, but remains continually concerned with his Creation.

Within this perspective it may be asked whether there is any need for Creation to have taken place at a particular instant of time. Is it not possible for the universe to have existed from all eternity in its state of complete dependence on its Creator? There are some philosophical and scientific reasons against the eternity of the universe, but there does not seem to be any specifically theological objection to this possibility.

134

If we believe in Creation at a particular instant of time, we do so because God has revealed it to us.

The traditional philosophical arguments for the existence of a Creator do not, of course, depend on particular scientific theories of the universe. They are based on simple everyday experiences of order in the world, and of the dependent nature of material things. Nevertheless the desire, already mentioned, to integrate our scientific and our theological knowledge into a coherent whole does provide an extra-scientific criterion for preferring some theories of the universe more than others. Thus if we believe from revelation that the universe was created at a particular instant of time, we must notice that this is more readily brought into coherence with scientific theories that describe the development of the universe from a unique beginning than with those that maintain that it has always existed. Thus Christians might be expected to favour such theories, while others might for similar reasons prefer the alternative steady state or oscillating universe theories.

These preferences run as hidden, and sometimes not so hidden, threads through all the scientific discussions of the origin of the universe. When they do come to the surface they are mentioned as feelings rather than as argued conclusions. Thus Hoyle remarks: 'In the older theories all the matter in the Universe is supposed to have appeared at one instant in time, the whole creation process taking the form of one big bang. For myself I find this idea very much queerer than continuous creation.'[26] He also found the big bang theory unacceptable on scientific grounds because it postulates an irrational process that cannot be described in scientific terms, and on philosophical grounds because it lies in principle beyond the realm of observation. Irrespective of its success, 'it simply cannot be a good scientific theory. Under no circumstances ought anything that sounds like a cosmic beginning be acquiesced in by the scientist.'[27] Another cosmologist, Harrison, recoiled from the evidence that the universe will keep expanding for ever as a 'Horrible thought' that 'would make the whole universe meaningless'.[28] Marxist-Leninist writers naturally reject the notion of an absolute beginning as fundamentally incompatible with the principles of dialectical materialism. Thus Sviderskii rejected the big bang theory as 'an unscientific popish conclusion'.[29]

While some Christians have indeed used the big bang theory as evidence for Creation, others have been more cautious, notably the

135

originator of the theory, the Belgian Abbé Lemaître, a Catholic priest. Modern Christian writers on cosmology realize very clearly that it is quite unwarranted to argue from a scientific theory, however successful, to a theological belief. It is always hazardous to make links of this character, as has been found very often in the development of science.

Now that Christians have realized that it is unwise to argue from the success of the big bang theory to the fact of Creation, and agnostics have seen the steady state and oscillating universe theories subjected to severe criticism on scientific grounds, the arena of argument has shifted. Theists now like to point to the singularity of the universe as evidence of its origin in a free act of the Creator, while agnostics tend to emphasize its necessary character, and therefore its lack of need for a Creator.

THE SCIENCE OF THE COSMOS

It is one of the most astonishing achievements of man that he is able by means of mathematical equations to probe the extremes of the very small and the very large, the recesses of the atomic nucleus and the vastness of cosmic space and time.

The work of the nineteenth-century astronomers showed that our sun is a rather ordinary star in one of the spiral arms of a galaxy of about 200 thousand million stars that we see in faint outline as the Milky Way. Billions of similar galaxies are visible in all directions, and in 1924 Hubble found that the frequency of the light from them is shifted in a way which shows that they are all moving rapidly away from us. Furthermore, the greater the distance from us the faster they are receding. In other words, all the galaxies are now moving in just the way we would expect if they had all come from a mighty explosion about ten thousand million years ago.

A deeper understanding of this expansion of the universe was provided by Einstein's general theory of relativity. His cosmological model was shown to lead to the observed expansion, and Lemaître derived from it the measured velocity of recession of the galaxies. Thus theory and experiment combine to support the idea that what we now see is an ageing universe, the scattered ashes and sparks remaining from the compressed incandescence of its fiery beginning.

Several other lines of evidence, such as the motions of clusters of galaxies and the relative proportions of various types of nuclei, also give the same result for the time when all the matter of the universe was concentrated in a small volume. We can apply the laws to physics to understand many of the processes occurring during the expansion of the universe from this initial compressed state, but at present there seems no possibility of finding out by scientific means what happened before the expansion began. It seems to be the ultimate limit of science, a singularity that some have ventured to call the Creation.

It must, however, be emphasized again that this is not a scientific inference. It is not possible to show scientifically of any state that there can be no antecedent state. We cannot exclude the possibility that there was a previous state, perhaps one of contraction. It has been suggested that the universe is eternal, either remaining always more or less the same on a sufficiently large scale, or perhaps alternately expanding and contracting. These theories will now be discussed in more detail.

There are several theories of the origin of the universe. The big bang theory considers the development of the universe as a continuous progression from an explosive beginning to a silent end. Quite recently, the actual processes occurring in the first few instants of this expansion have been reconstructed in considerable detail, making use of the latest knowledge of nuclear and elementary particle physics. The arguments are highly technical and still somewhat speculative for the very earliest times, namely the first fraction of a second. After this, the course of development is understood in some detail, and research is continually providing more information, even of the processes occurring in the first hundredth of a second. Before then nuclei did not exist, and to trace the evolution further back we need the results of elementary particle physics. The earliest time envisaged is the Planck time, 10^{-43} seconds after the singularity, when all the matter in the universe, comprising thousands of millions of galaxies, was compressed within a sphere of radius one-thousandth of a centimetre, the size of the point of a needle. The density was then about 10^{90} kilograms per cc. One astronomer has remarked: 'These conditions are so extreme that it is entirely appropriate to regard the Planck time as the moment of creation of the universe'.[30] In saying this, he goes beyond science, and yet this itself shows how modern science insistently forces such questions upon us, questions that can only receive a theological answer.

It is worth noting the extreme specificity of the whole process, a feature that will be returned to later on. In particular the ratio of nuclear particles to photons, electrons and neutrinos must be about one to a thousand million. If there are more photons the number of neutrons and protons will remain about the same, so that as soon as the temperature falls low enough for helium to be formed, they will all combine in this way. Nearly all the nuclear particles will become helium, and then it is not possible to build up any of the heavier nuclei. On the other hand, if there are fewer photons the interaction that keeps the number of neutrons and protons the same will cease too soon, and before the helium formation can begin, most of the neutrons will have decayed to protons. Nearly all the nuclear particles will then be protons, and so not enough helium can be formed to lead to the production of heavier nuclei. Thus the ratio is exceedingly critical; if it is too large or too small there can be no nuclei heavier than helium, and so no possibility of life.

As an alternative to the big bang theory, Bondi and Gold, and also Hoyle, proposed the steady state theory in 1948. This was based on what they called the Perfect Cosmological Principle, which says that on a sufficiently large scale the universe is always the same, both in space and in time. In particular, the number of galaxies in any large volume of space is constant. Since, however, we know that the galaxies are receding from each other, this can only be ensured if new galaxies are coming into being to replace those that are moving away. They therefore postulated that hydrogen atoms continually appear out of nothing and ultimately condense and coalesce to form new galaxies at a rate just sufficient to replace those lost by recession. The rate of appearance came out to be so small that there is no possibility of ever observing it, just one hydrogen atom per year in every cubic mile of space.

The motivation behind this theory was avowedly to provide a rival to the big bang theory. To do this, they were obliged to postulate what they called continuous creation, yet they resolutely refused to consider how this creation occurred, or to attribute it to a Creator. It thus seemed to many to be a somewhat gratuitous hypothesis, and yet they were correct to maintain that it is a legitimate scientific theory that stands or falls when its consequences are compared with observational data.

The most direct test of the theory is to see if indeed the galaxies are uniformly spread throughout all space. At first this seemed to be the case; the number of galaxies increased as the cube of the distance, as it should. However, it has now been found by the techniques of radioastronomy that at very large distances the galaxies start thinning out; there are not enough of them for the steady state theory to be correct. Further evidence against the steady state theory is provided by the observation of the background radiation, which shows that the present expansion of the universe started some ten thousand million years ago. For these reasons the steady state theory has now been abandoned, and scientists reluctant to envisage the possibility of a Creation turned their attention to the theory of an oscillating universe.

At present the universe is expanding, but the question is whether is will go on expanding for ever, the galaxies and the stars getting colder and colder, or whether at some epoch the expansion will slow down and go into reverse, leading eventually to the collapse of the universe into a very small volume. If the universe is ultimately destined to collapse we can then see the present expansion and collapse may be just one of a whole series of expansions and contractions, going on for ever, a spectacle that banishes the possibility of a Creation at a particular instant but not, it must be added, the need for a continuing Sustainer of the whole oscillating process.

There are some scientific difficulties with the possibility of an oscillating universe, but it cannot yet be ruled out. Scientifically, it remains an open question.

Philosophically, an eternal oscillating universe is open to the objection that if we are in such a universe then everything would already have happened an infinite time ago. The only way to avoid this conclusion is to say that the whole of history is indeed repeated in all its details an infinite number of times. The periodicity of this repetition need not be the same as that of the universe as a whole, providing it is equal or greater. Such a belief in an oscillating universe has indeed often occurred in human history, and indeed is a ubiquitous feature of ancient cultures. Its debilitating effects played no small part in preventing the rise of science in all those cultures, as shown in detail in Jaki's book *Science and Creation*. In the Judeo-Christian civilization this idea was rejected because the incarnation of Christ is a unique event that cannot be repeated; God's plan in history is a linear one, from the beginning to the end, and it is incompatible with eternally recurring cycles. That is why the Church has always believed in

Creation in time, and conversely it is notable that belief in an oscillating universe is always one of the hallmarks of atheism.

THE SINGULARITY OF THE UNIVERSE

The more closely scientists study the evolution of the universe the more evidence they find of its extreme singularity. A striking example of this has already been quoted: if the proportions of nuclear particles and photons had been slightly different there would have been nearly all hydrogen or nearly all helium, and in each case no heavier nuclei and so no possibility of life. Again, it has been noted that the universe is remarkable homogeneous on a large scale, and this is a result of the initial conditions. It is very difficult to understand why these inhomogeneities should be so small, yet if they were any larger the matter of the universe would have collapsed into black holes long ago, while if they had been any smaller, there would have been no galaxies.

The evolution of the solar system is also highly specific. There is still no satisfactory theory of how the system of planets was formed, and in particular how they came to be rotating round the sun in nearly circular orbits, and nearly in the same plane. Yet it is only on a planet of a certain size moving on a nearly circular orbit, that life could have evolved. The more this evolution is studied, the more we realize that it is immensely improbable that we should be here at all. The universe has evolved along a very narrow path, indeed just the path that makes man possible. That is why we can say that it is *our* universe. Freeman Dyson has summed this up in the words: 'As we look out into the universe and identify the many accidents of physics and astronomy that have worked together to our benefit, it almost seems as if the universe must in some sense have known that we were coming.'[31] This connection between man and the universe restores man to a central place in the universe in a far deeper sense than that discredited by the Copernican revolution.

Man always tends naturally to think that he is in the centre of all things. The ancient Hebrew cosmology, the cosmology of the Greeks, the cosmology of the Hindus all put man in the centre of the universe. In Genesis man appears as God's supreme handiwork on the sixth day, and all creation is his to dominate. This anthropocentric picture received a crushing blow when Copernicus showed that the motions of the planets can be much better understood if they rotate about the sun, so now the sun is in the centre, with the earth a rather small planet revolving round it. Man's centrality received further blows when it was shown that the sun, so impressive to us, is a rather undistinguished star near the end of a spiral arm of a vast galaxy of billions of such stars, and that this galaxy is but one of many billions of similar galaxies scattered throughout an unimaginably large universe. At the end of this man looks very insignificant indeed, even if he can comfort himself with the words of Pascal about his knowing the universe that does not know him.

And now, when we know far more about the universe, when we begin to understand in a very detailed way the evolution of the very matter of which it is composed, we begin at the same time to glimpse a new truth, that it looks more and more as if the universe was indeed made just for man. At each stage in its development there seem to be many possibilities, and every time the one is chosen that alone leads to a universe that can produce man. Within this perspective the apparent insignificance of man takes on a completely different aspect. We wonder at the vastness of the universe in space and in time compared with the smallness and frailty of man. Why this apparent prodigality? Now we glimpse the answer; all that stupendous evolution was necessary in order that the earth should be made as a habitation for man. The process of nucleosynthesis, by which the elements constituting man's body are built up in the interior of stars, takes billions of years. And in this time the galaxies containing these stars will inevitably move vast distances from their point of formation. So the universe must be as large and as old as it is in order that it can be prepared as a home for man.

The idea that the universe has taken just that path in its evolution that leads to man is called the anthropic principle.[32] It must be noted that this principle does not explain why the universe evolved in this particular way, unless we already believe in a Creator who intended this result. Since we are indeed here, then of course the universe must be such as to allow our emergence. If the universe had, so to speak, taken the wrong turning, then we would not be here to talk about it. Or perhaps there have been millions of different universes in non-interacting spaces, and this is just the one that happened to be such as to allow the evolution of man. We may or may not think that these arguments are plausible, but they are certainly tenable.

It is unquestionable that the advances of modern science have given us an astonishingly detailed knowledge of the evolution of the physical universe from that singular instant of time about ten thousand million years ago to the present time. Unlike the cosmology of the Hebrews, which was pre-scientific speculation, modern cosmology is real knowledge that will endure. Certainly we will continue to understand the process in more and more detail; in particular we will obtain in the next few years a greater understanding of the fundamental interactions occurring in the first hundredth of a second. The subsequent evolution will be understood in more precise detail, with more accurate numbers for the proportions of the various types of fundamental particles. Further evidence of singularities may well be found, and links between them may be found to show their necessary character. In a few decades, our knowledge of the universe may well make our present understanding look puny by comparison. But in spite of this the broad outlines of our cosmology will remain, just as the mechanics of Newton still remains valid in its proper domain.

The story of man's developing understanding of the cosmos has always been strongly affected by his fundamental beliefs, in particular by his belief in a Creator. As we have seen, the relationship between his scientific and theological beliefs is not a simple one, certainly not one that allows a compelling deduction from one to the other. It is not possible to use scientific theories, however well supported, to construct an argument for a Creator, and neither can they be used to render his existence superfluous.

From a purely scientific point of view the atheist and the agnostic are free to pursue their research in the hope of demonstrating the oscillatory structure of the universe and to reduce the evidences of singularity by finding necessary connections. Indeed these are activities in which theistic scientists will share, knowing that whatever is found by scientific research will ultimately show forth in ever more compelling detail the creative power of God.

These believers, convinced on other grounds that the universe originated by divine fiat at an instant of time, will view our present knowledge of its evolution in a different perspective. The Christian belief in Creation is in complete harmony with the idea that the universe came into being at a singular instant about ten thousand million years ago, or perhaps at an earlier singular instant, and subsequently developed in the way described by modern scientific cosmology. The whole vast process is controlled and designed by

God's creative power with the intention of producing man, the crown of his Creation, a being made in his own image and likeness, endowed with free-will and consciousness, and the ability to understand the processes that brought him into being.

Within this perspective we can see the process as an integrated whole, shot through with very purposeful activity. We are not insignificant specks generated by some chance process in an alien universe. On the contrary, the whole process, stretching over billions of years and vast unimaginable spaces, was designed and intended precisely to bring us into existence with the power to know and love our Creator.

NOTES

1   S. L. Jaki, *Science and Creation* (Edinburgh 1974).
2   A. N. Whitehead, *Science and the Modern World* (Cambridge 1926), p. 19.
3   Further discussion of the relation of Marxism to science may be found in *The Relevance of Physics* by S. L. Jaki (Chicago 1966), ch. 11. This chapter has been used in preparing the present essay.
4   F. Engels, *Dialectics of Nature*, trans. C. Dutt (New York 1940), p. 243.
5   V. I. Lenin, *Materialism and Empirico-Criticism* (New York 1927), p. 323.
6   N. I. Bukharin, quoted in Jaki, *The Relevance of Physics* (Chicago 1966), p. 487.
7   A. A. Zhdanov, quoted in Jaki, *The Relevance of Physics*, p. 488.
8   I. V. Kuznetsov, quoted in Jaki, *The Relevance of Physics*, p. 485.
9   John R. Baker, *Science and the Planned State* (London 1945).
10 See also P. E. Hodgson, 'Philosophical Implications of Quantum Physics', *Proceedings* of the 8th International Wittgenstein Symposium (Vienna 1984), p. 237.
11 Karl R. Popper, *Quantum Theory and the Schism in Physics*, ed. W. W. Bartley III, (London 1982), p. 95.
12 W. Heisenberg, *Daedalus*, 87.95 (1958).
13 Karl R. Popper, *op. cit.*, p. 9.
14 A. Einstein, *The World as I See It* (London 1935), p. 156.
15 A. Einstein, in *Albert Einstein, Philosopher-Scientist*, ed. P. Schilpp (Cambridge 1970), p. 21.
16 Karl R. Popper, *op. cit.*, p. 46.
17 Lord Rayleigh, *The Life of Sir J. J. Thomson* (Cambridge 1942), p. 265.
18 J. von Neumann, *Mathematical Foundations of Quantum Mechanics* (Berlin 1932).
19 C. A. Hooker, article in *Contemporary Research in the Foundations and Philosophy of Quantum Theory*, ed. C. A. Hooker (Dordrecht 1973).

20   John Polkinghorne, *The Way the World Is* (London 1983), p. 5.
21   Karl R. Popper, *op. cit.*, p. 57.
22   William G. Pollard, *Chance and Providence* (New York 1958).
23   For the realist interpretation of science, see Roy Bhaskar, *A Realist Theory of Science* (Brighton 1978); Richard Healey (ed.), *Reduction, Time and Reality* (Cambridge 1981); 'Scientific Realism', *Philosophical Quarterly*, 32 (July 1982).
24   B. Pascal, *Pensées*, lxxxvii.
25   Margaret Knight, *Science in its Context*, ed. John Brierley (London 1964), p. 126.
26   F. Hoyle, *Astronomy and Cosmology* (Oxford 1975), p. 684.
27   F. Hoyle, *The Nature of the Universe* (Oxford 1950), p. 105.
28   E. R. Harrison, quoted in Jaki, *The Road of Science and the Ways to God* (Chicago 1978), p. 272.
29   E. McMullin, *The Sciences and Theology in the Twentieth Century*, ed. A. R. Peacocke (Stocksfield 1981), p. 17.
30   J. Silk, *The Big Bang* (Oxford 1980), p. 104.
31   Freeman J. Dyson, *(Scientific American*, 225.25 (1971).
32   For discussion of the anthropic principle, see B. J. Carr, 'On the Origin, Purpose and Evolution of the Physical Universe', *Irish Astronomical Journal*, 15.237 (1982); B. J. Carr and M. J. Rees, 'The Anthropic Principle and the Structure of the Physical World', *Nature*, 278.605 (1979); P. C. W. Davies, *The Accidental Universe* (Cambridge 1982); S. L. Jaki, *Cosmos and Creator* (Edinburgh 1980).

4 Christianity and the Passing Age

JAMES MUNSON

In the last year of the nineteenth century the President of the Baptist Union, the Revd William Cuff, told the audience at the Union's spring session:[1]

> We are leaving behind us a century of the most colossal progress the world has ever witnessed, throughout the Empire and all over the world . . . There are locks now for which there are no keys, but the keys will be made that will fit the locks, and doors will be opened, and more amazing treasures will be found . . . This is no dream of a fond and overweening faith, for it is based on the solid facts of the past, as well as on the covenant promises of our living Lord. . . The nineteenth century is the one great epoch of discovery; not only in political and social developments, but also in general progress in art and science, leaving behind it all other centuries.

Fifteen years later Gunner John Cudlip of the 108th Heavy Battery, Royal Garrison Artillery, wrote to a friend in Britain during a lull in the Second Battle of Ypres: 'Dear Miss Christie, there is no doubt a great slaughter has taken place during last week. I should like to be able to get a good sleep, we have only had two or three hours rest during the bombardment, for it has been on night and day. . . it makes one wonder if Europe is really civilised after all.'[2]

THE COLLAPSE OF INEVITABLE HUMAN PROGRESS

The fifteen years between Mr Cuff's speech and Gunner Cudlip's letter mark the collapse of the idea of progress, of progress, that is, as an inevitable fixture and logical outcome of British life and history. Progress is, of course, the name some people give to a sequence of events which they approve because they feel that these events and this sequence improve the quality of life or advance the obtaining of a goal they desire. What constitutes progress to some is what others find a sad tale of decline from previously held beliefs or a previous state of existence.

The idea of progress can soon become a touchstone applied to changes by those who wish others to accept them. It was against this that the historian Jacob Burckhardt complained: 'Our dear nineteenth century has so accustomed people to the idea that everything new, however questionable in itself, is justified, that nothing can any longer hinder the process. It is quite incredible how empty-headed and defenceless even thoroughly decent people are when confronted by the spirit of the age.'[3] One is reminded of the slogan used by America's General Electric Corporation: 'Progress is our most important product.'

Victorians would have excused themselves from Burckhardt's censure. When they defined progress they normally did so, in the first instance, by reference back to English history, to the steady unfolding of a great story. This story was of the development of a free, Protestant nation founded on an open Bible at the Reformation, a purified Church, parliamentary government, a limited monarchy, the rule of law through independent courts, the abolition of restrictions on trade, commerce, journalism, literature and personal freedom, expanding franchise and, in their own century, massive efforts to extend education and to lift the masses in preparation for the democracy that was bound to come in the twentieth century. John Cassell's *Illustrated History of England*, sold in weekly penny numbers and aimed at the working man, said simply that 'it has been the august mission of Great Britain, under Providence, to exhibit the principles of human government in their most exalted form'. The historian's task was 'to record the growth and achievement of our own country by the sure though gradual development amongst the people themselves of sound social and political principles'.[4] The national achievement was political, religious and individual freedom combined with a strong social cohesiveness. We tend to forget, or rather to take for granted, that British history has been for several centuries, a happy one. If we compare it to that of Poland, or Ireland, or the Balkans or, indeed, to that of France for many years, we see the difference.

The second point of reference that the Victorians used to define progress was the tremendous improvement in the quality of life about them. These improvements sustained the inherited Whig view of history outlined above, and carried it into the new technological age. Victorians coped amazingly well with the greatest fact of their age: by 1851 the majority, at least of Englishmen, no longer lived on the land but in cities. England had become an urban civilization with urban problems. But the list of achievements in meeting these problems is still impressive: housing, health, transportation, factory legislation, literacy, sanitation, education, public libraries – what William Cuff, addressing his fellow Baptists in 1900, referred to as 'the solid facts of the past'. English society had proved itself supple enough to accommodate these changes within existing structures. It was also inventive enough to create new structures where necessary to supplement the old, as in local government.

The collapse of the idea of progress is normally traced to the effects on popular views of the Great War with its tremendous blood-letting. But informed opinion had been worried for several decades before 1914 about the resilience of British institutions and about Britain's position in the world. The problems were many: the problem of Irish self-government and the threat of civil war in Ireland in 1914; the rise of civil unrest in England as seen in the militant suffragettes; a series of industrial strikes; growing competition in industry from Germany and the United States; the isolation in which Britain found herself during the South African War (1899–1902) and, finally the discovery, of which we shall see more later, that cities bred a more intractable species of poverty than had been thought.

The idea of progress is being examined here in order to understand the Church's present secularization. In historical terms, secularization is not new. It has happened to the Christian Church before, in eighteenth-century France or nineteeth-century Russia. Also, of course, secularization is not so much a static situation as a question of degree based on a necessary amount of interplay between the Church and the particular society in which the Church is found. Secularization is a question of excess, of having too much of what Professor David Martin calls 'the wider community'.[5]

No Church could exist if it were not to some degree associated with the society in which it is located. It must, as it were, speak the same language. It must share to some degree the same history and the same values of its society. When this relationship extends over the centuries, as it has in England or France or Ethiopia, a complex network of relationships and shared experiences is built up. (At some stages it is crucial in the

147

nation's history: in England such a stage occurred at the Trial of the Bishops under James II.) In Poland today the Church embodies the spirit of a non-communist, Christian people under a communist régime; in Russia the Orthodox Church remains the one link with Russian history and culture before the Bolshevik Revolution and in Ethiopia the Coptic Church links the people with their pre-Marxist history, hence the desire of the government to destroy the Church.

This identity is not secularization, for neither partner imposes on the other, or detracts from the other's identity or work. For the Church of England to be English, the Polish Church to be Polish, the Russian Church to be Russian or the Coptic Church to be Ethiopian does not detract from the Church's ability to preach the Gospel or dispense the Sacraments. Secularization is a question of impinging to the point of taking over. It presumes a 'secular' society at odds with the Church's teaching. Our task is to trace the development of this 'secular' society in England, which begins in the early nineteenth century. What we need to do is to look at certain strands in our history to show how they have combined to create this 'secular' society which threatens to engulf the Church.

Let us first look at the Assize Sermon of John Keble, preached on 14 July 1833. When he came to publish the sermon, Keble gave it the title 'National Apostasy'. Apostasy from what? John Keble was defending the inherited view of history I have outlined before. Although he was a High-Churchman he nevertheless subscribed to the Whig view of England's history. Sociologists might today call this view a 'model', an England where Church and kingdom were one body, one people. To be English was to be Christian and to be English was to be part of the Church of England. There were, of course, exceptions, but the very fact that non-Anglican Christians were called 'dissenters' showed that the model still held, despite deviations. The fear that gripped John Keble was that the exceptions were about to alter the rules, to 'break the model'.

John Keble saw himself as a prophet and he chose as his text the twenty-third verse from 1 Samuel, chapter 12: 'God forbid that I should sin against the Lord in ceasing to pray for you: but I will teach you the good and the right way.' Samuel was denouncing the Jews because they were forsaking God's government by a demand for a king. Keble's task was to 'teach the good and the right way'. The 'national apostasy' which he felt was coming had a variety of causes. The most immediate one was, of course, the Church Temporalities (Ireland) Bill which had been given a Second Reading in the House of Commons nine weeks before. It had been put forward by the Whig administration of Lord Grey to pacify Catholic opinion in Ireland.

Since the Act of Union, the established Churches of England and Ireland were united into one Church. The one body which could legislate for this United Church was Parliament; convocations were not sitting and synods had yet to be thought up. Under the bill Irish bishoprics were to be reduced from twenty-two to twelve; church lands were to be taken over by laymen and ancient church taxes abolished. What could be done to the Irish Church to pacify Catholics could be done to the English Church to pacify Dissenters. (With regard to Ireland, Keble was on rather thin ice because history and custom, which united the English people and Church, did not do so across St George's Channel: only twenty out of every 100 Irishmen were members of the Established Church.)

To John Keble this bill was but the latest in an unprecedented attack on the 'ancient constitution in Church and State'. In 1828 Parliament, hitherto the guardian of this constitution, began dismantling it bit by bit when it repealed the Test and Corporation Acts. Dissenters could now sit in Parliament and participate in local government. In 1829, again to gain peace in Ireland, the Duke of Wellington's administration put through the Catholic Emancipation Act. This meant that Roman Catholics could also sit in Parliament. In 1832 Lord Grey put through the great Reform Bill after months of rioting, much of it directed against the Church, by mobs inspired by radical, and often republican, orators. In Bristol the Bishop's palace was burned to the ground by rioters.

Even more threatening was the new political alliance of Whigs– Dissenters–Radicals which had supporters even among churchmen like Thomas Arnold, the spiritual father of those who are for ever wondering how the Church can best accommodate herself to the unspoken demands of an unnumbered crowd. Thomas Arnold followed the Erastian light: what Parliament had 'made', Parliament could alter. He wanted legislation to incorporate Dissenters into the Church by the simple ploy of altering doctrine. Others thought it would be nice to abolish the Creeds, at least in public worship where they were said to give offence. Some thought it a good idea to get rid of the Trinity to win over the Unitarians, or to abolish the doctrine of baptismal regeneration and the use of priestly absolution.

To Keble there was another question lurking beyond the immediate one: if the English Church were attacked, if the ancient foundations of a Christian kingdom were undermined and a new non-Christian nation created on its ruins, could English Christianity survive? Could such a nation claim to be Christian with a legislature freed from the old restraints, to legislate against natural law and divine teaching? This is what John Keble said:

> What are the symptoms by which one may judge most fairly whether or not a nation as such is becoming alienated from God and Christ? The case is at least possible of a nation, having for centuries acknowledged as an essential part of its theory of government, that as a Christian nation she is also part of Christ's Church and bound in all her legislation and policy by the fundamental rules of that Church, deliberately throwing off the restraint which, in many respects such a principle would impose on them, nay, disavowing the principle itself.

Keble next turned to 'the impatient patrons of innovations' and the 'fashionable liberality of this generation'. Such 'patrons' were anxious to appease the Dissenters' demands for 'religious liberty'. But behind this willingness to appease the Dissenters was another question – indifference:

> One of the most alarming symptoms is the growing indifference in which men indulge themselves to other men's religious sentiments. Under the guise of charity and tolerance we are come almost to this pass; that no difference in matters of faith is to disqualify for our approbation and confidence, whether in public or domestic life. I do not speak of things thought to become, from time to time, necessary; but I speak of the spirit which leads men to exult in every step of that kind; to congratulate one another on the supposed decay of what they call an 'exclusive system'.

This 'supposed decay of what they call an "exclusive system"' became the very foundation of Victorian England. None of the many changes in English life which the nineteenth century produced has had so far-reaching and permanent an effect as the abolition in fact, if not in theory, of the 'ancient constitution in Church and State'.[6] The fight for what has been called an 'open' society, had already begun before Keble spoke. Nonconformists in Birmingham had already begun withholding church rates; the Political Union of Glasgow had petitioned the House of Lords to exclude bishops from the upper house and there was talk about legislation to allow civil marriage and the entry of Dissenters into Oxford and Cambridge.

The nineteenth century would see much more: burial acts allowed Nonconformist ministers to hold services in churchyards; Jews and eventually atheists were allowed to sit in the House of Commons; civil marriage was followed in time by divorce legislation. In our own century, this development has shown itself in questions of personal morality, with legislation legalizing adult homosexual acts in private, and allowing the abortion of unborn children. Morality, that is, the 'rightness' and 'wrongness' of an act, increasingly depend not on whether such acts violate the Church's teaching or the natural law, what Keble called the 'fundamental rules', but on whether or not the individual taking the decision can justify it by reference to some personal ethical standard.

The divorce between traditional morality as defined by the Church and present morality is not a product of the 'permissive society'. It is a logical outcome of the changes brought about by the Victorians in their adherence to the idea of progress. Once the old alliance of Church and State had begun to crumble, a new 'secular' world was being gradually created. Most of the people devoted to this new view of society were Christian and would have denied most strenuously that any conflict between their religious faith and the new social order was either inherent or inevitable. But such a conflict was inevitable. In our own time, it has led to the view that England is not a Christian nation at all.

THE CULT OF INDIVIDUAL LIBERTY

There is a second strand which has helped to create our modern 'secular' society and which followed on the collapse of John Keble's world. The Victorian proponents of the new social order needed a new creed. They found this creed, as far as morality and social ethics were concerned, in the works of the man whom Mr Gladstone called 'the saint of rationalism', John Stuart Mill. Mill once wrote that 'I was brought up from the first without any religious belief'.[7] Like many intellectuals, he confused 'religious belief' with 'belief' and of the latter he had a sufficient quota. His greatest belief was in the value of individual liberty. In his essay *On Liberty* he discussed 'the nature and limits of the power which can be legitimately exercised by society over the individual'. Gone were the teachings of the Church, gone were eighteen hundred years of tradition and experience, gone were the inhibitions of natural and divine law. 'Liberty', he wrote, 'consists in doing what one desires', a specious enough assertion to win converts over the years. Likewise, he said, 'all restraint, *qua* restraint, is an evil.'

Mill admitted, however, that individuals can be constrained, either by law or by public opinion. Mill himself had never been unduly constrained in the affair he had conducted for twenty-one years with another man's wife, so public opinion did not account for too much. What was left was the power of the State, of the new 'secular' State. This State, he argued, could limit a subject's liberty on one specific ground:[8]

> When, in short, there is a definite damage, or a definite risk of damage, either to an individual or to the public, the case is taken out of the province of liberty, and placed in that of morality or law. But with regard to the merely contingent, or, it may be called, constructive injury which a person causes to society, by conduct which neither violates any specific duty to the public, nor occasions perceptible hurt to any assignable individual except himself; the inconvenience is one which society can afford to bear, for the sake of the greater good of human freedom.

Translated into non-Utilitarian English, this means that an individual may do whatever he wants so long as no other individual or the public is 'damaged'. Thus, one can argue, to kill oneself is permissible because there is no 'definitive damage' to another – only the inconvenience of a shattered home and a body to be disposed of: such is the logical extent to which Mill's teaching has been put.

When one is younger, there is much in Mill's writing that attracts: the cult of the individual is never so strong as in those years between getting a place at university and getting a place in the mortgage queue. As one grows in sense one discovers that, even if God, natural law, divine law, tradition and revealed religion are disregarded, there is no such thing as a wholly 'individual' act. Even so, Mill's writings have influenced millions of Englishmen who have never heard his name.

Individual freedom – the liberty of the subject – had long been one of England's greatest boasts. Now it had taken on a moral character. I recall a woman interviewed on television. Her local vicar had dared to say that there might be something wrong in so many women having fewer children and smaller families if it was in order to have larger incomes and longer holidays. Her reply would have pleased 'the saint of rationalism': 'It's a bit too much', she said, 'when the Church tries to interfere in family life.'

Pluralism rules. Again, we may recall the habitual valediction of the television comedian, Dave Allen: 'May your god go with you.' We should have a god, but we should choose which one we want. We should, and do, have a hospital ward in which are two women. The one is undergoing extensive treatment in order to have a baby while the other is waiting for an abortion: the gods differ but at least each is free to choose.

HOW CHURCHMEN ADAPT

What is interesting is the manner in which churchmen come to terms with the advancing secular society. The teaching of the atheist, Mill, eventually found its way into quite a few clergymen's writings. I shall cite one. Canon Samuel Barnett, President of Toynbee Hall, preached in Westminster Abbey in 1911. He said:[9]

> The English Nation, by the influences of race, of geographical position and of experience, has developed certain prominent characteristics, or in other language has been specially called for the establishment and exaltation of freedom within its own borders and in the world. This call is thus a call from God, and as a co-operator with God, England is constrained by its laws and its policy to make clear the way for freedom, just as Israel was constrained to make clear the way for righteousness. Religion requires that the laws and the policy of England shall be directed against such enemies to freedom as those with which I have dealt in these lectures [pauperism, luxury, drunkenness, impurity, ignorance and war].

The moral imperative to individual freedom has now become a gift from God and this, not the demands of the Christian religion, is the motive for social action.

My argument so far has been that the destruction of John Keble's world by the economic, social and political changes of the nineteenth century left a vacuum. This vacuum was filled by the creation of a new social morality based on excessive devotion to individual liberty and Progress in intellectual as well as material matters. This new attitude demanded a 'neutral' state which would destroy the old assumption of a 'Christian' nation on which the Church–State alliance had been formulated at the Reformation. The problem was not limited to England. In France or Italy the battle was much sharper and in France the Church eventually came to accept the 'secular state' in the papal epistle, *Au Milieu des Sollicitudes* of 1892. For the Church of England the battle was much less fierce because of the role of English Nonconformity, which forms the third strand in those forces which have created our secular world.

To many people today, Nonconformity means the disused chapels now converted, if that is the right word, into off-licences, shops and private homes. The decline of Nonconformity as a major factor in our national life has been a water-shed but little noticed by historians concerned with religion only in so far as it affects politics. The vacuum left by Nonconformity's decline has been increasingly filled by the Roman Catholic Church as it has moved out of its 'Irish ghetto' into the mainstream of national life. One example will show what I mean: in the autumn of 1984 a fund was established to help the families of those miners on strike. The news bulletins said the fund was being established by the Bishop of Liverpool and the Roman Catholic Archbishop of Liverpool. It was not thought worthwhile, by most journalists, to mention that the third trustee was the Moderator of the Free Church Federal Council.

NONCONFORMITY AND THE VICTORIAN SPIRIT

Yet, the importance of Nonconformity has been crucial. I must here trace certain historical changes. In the nineteenth century, Nonconformity underwent major changes. The five major Methodist groups moved slowly towards unity although this was not finally achieved until the 1930s. Methodists also began to see themselves as 'Nonconformists', a description many would have rejected at one time. The changing attitude was due to the growth of High-Church power within the Church of England. The older Dissenters (Congregationalists and

Baptists along with Presbyterians to a lesser degree) abandoned almost universally their adherence to Calvinism. Nonconformity was therefore in flux, like society as a whole. It quickly became identified with the new Victorian culture. If the Church of England never really recovered from urbanization, the Nonconformists thrived on it. A higher proportion of Nonconformists lived in urban areas than the population generally. Nonconformity came to terms with the new learning of Spencer, Darwin and Mill relatively easily. It benefited enormously from the social advancement of the upper-working classes and the lower-middle classes through increased state intervention in education. Indeed, the 1870 Education Act, which established for the first time state elementary schools, created a new type of religious education – 'nondenominational' to placate opposing forces. At first, Nonconformists had wanted no religious education in state schools: religion should be left to the churches. But they quickly realized the enormous potential in the new approach which would help them to create a Christian, but not an Anglican England.

Nonconformity's power was enormous. By the end of the century its major denominations constituted over half the total number of active members of all non-Roman Catholic churches in England. Nonconformist Sunday schools reached over three and a quarter million children. Nonconformist buildings changed the face of England and Wales while Nonconformist names permeated every aspect of Victorian England: Lloyds and Barclays banks, Wills tobacco, Firth steel, Rank flour (and later films), Mackintosh sweets, Lever soaps, Reckitt's blueing, Clark shoes, Colman's mustard, Wall's sausages, Beecham's powders; jams by Hartley, Wilkins or Chivers, sweets by Callard, sugar from Tate, ten-guinea tours from Cook's, matches from Bryant and May, glass from Pilkington, thread from Clark or Coats, carpets from Crossley, hats from Christy, silks from Courtauld's, books from James Clarke, Cassell, Hodder & Stoughton or Allen & Unwin, medicines from Boots, chocolates from Fry, Storr, Rowntree or Cadbury – all four were Quaker firms. Even the new American competitor, Hershey, whose product is said to resemble chocolate, was a Nonconformist. In law, journalism, and literature Nonconformists had become powerful forces by the end of the Victorian era. In politics, England had her first Nonconformist Prime Minister in 1908 when Asquith took office and after him, Lloyd George, Bonar Law and Ramsay Macdonald were all, more or less, Nonconformists.

It was Nonconformity, far more than the Church of England, which embodied the Victorian spirit. It was the serious minded, highly principled, individualistic, evangelical, Bible-based descendants of the Puritans who shaped Victorian culture. Matthew Arnold might decry their 'provincialism' but he also gave a grudging admiration to their doctrine of individualism:[10]

> Having, I say, at the bottom of our English hearts a very strong belief in freedom, and a very weak belief in right reason, we are soon silenced when a man pleads the prime right to do as he likes, because this is the prime right for ourselves too. . .

But Nonconformity is a question of law, not of religious faith. A man was only a 'nonconformist' because he was a Baptist or a Congregationalist, not the other way round. What law made, law could unmake, hence the perennial cry for 'disestablishment'. As Nonconformist ministers became better educated their sensibility increased, as is often the case. But their new status was not recognized by 'the establishment'. It is not surprising that they frequently turned to the great 'puritan republic' across the Atlantic, a nation where the establishment of any religion was expressly forbidden in the Constitution. In America there was no such thing as Nonconformity. Back in England the cry became 'religious equality' as religious liberty became an accepted aspect of life.

THE STRUGGLE TO REGAIN THE CENTRE

This inherent proneness to political awareness, the undeniable strength and vibrancy of Nonconformity and the example of America combined inexorably towards greater political involvement. But the minister, priest or, indeed, even bishop, who ventures into the political arena is like the reformer who enters the house of ill-fame: he walks in to reform but he might stay to enjoy. The political world is a very tempting world, concerned as it is with grabbing and holding power. Politics stood at the very centre of the new secular society. This meant that churches, now reduced to voluntary bodies, were driven to the periphery. In order once again to be at the centre churches needed to conduct themselves in ways approved by the political centre. Nonconformists perfectly understood this, and again they looked to America, where the Protestant churches had got caught up in the debate over slavery. The Revd Henry Ward Beecher, like his sister, Harriet Beecher Stowe, became a famous leader in the intellectual circles of their day which pushed for abolition. His career only subsided after sexual scandals tarnished his image; his influence in Britain was enormous.

In England party politics gave Nonconformists a ready opportunity within the broad spectrum of the Liberal Party. But for those afraid of too close a party involvement, the 1880s opened a new avenue when the middle classes discovered the 'social problem'. Although now the very stuff of after-dinner talk, the social problem was innovatory in the 1880s. There was a virtual explosion of social investigation; explorers no longer needed Basutoland for they had found Bermondsey. In the concern for inner-urban poverty Nonconformists led the way. In 1883 Andrew Mearns, Secretary of the London Congregational Union, brought out 'The Bitter Cry of Outcast London'. In the 1890s it was Charles Booth, the son of Unitarian parents, who supervised his massive study, *Life and Labour of the People in London*. Seebohm Rowntree, famous for his study of York, *Poverty: A Study of Town Life*, was a Quaker who had left chocolate for sociology. It was William Booth of the Salvation Army who took up the cause of 're-colonizing' rural England with the urban poor in his book, *In Darkest England and the Way Out*, published in 1890. The problems were legion: rural decline, appalling urban poverty, underpaid workers, prostitution among children and the lack of adequate secondary education were but a few. It is not that the Nonconformists created this type of social investigation; it had been going on for some eighty years by the end of the last century. What is important is that Nonconformists, by conducting such investigations and expressing such concerns, showed themselves fully at one with intellectual thought.

The most important aspect of all this Nonconformist activity was the propagation of the 'social gospel', the ready application to 'social problems' of which there were now so many, of the Christian gospel. The difficulty was, then as now, that there were only so many possible solutions to any one problem. By the time the churches had got to the centre from their position on the periphery they usually found that someone else, usually a political party, had got there first. Some Nonconformist laymen protested against ministers who preached nothing but 'the latest theories of the. . . *Fortnightly* [*Review*] hashed up'.[11] Others, like the Congregational layman, J. Carvell Williams,

Liberal MP for Mansfield, were proud of the Nonconformists' political involvement. Nonconformity, he said, 'has exerted during the present century, and is still exerting, a constantly increasing force – a force that has to be reckoned with in legislature, in local government, and in matters affecting the moral interests of the community'. He could have added that Nonconformity's greatest political punch was felt in secret meetings of the Liberal Party's leadership.[12]

The 'social gospel' itself arose out of the shocked realization that Nonconformity's claim to be the church of the 'people' as opposed to the 'establishment' was groundless. Nonconformity was overwhelmingly middle-class and upper-working class and increasingly suburban as people left town centres for leafy suburbs. Rhetoric and reality had moved miles apart. Nonconformists, no less than the Church of England, had to appeal to the 'unchurched millions' who cared for neither very much. A Special Committee on the Work of the Churches reported to the Congregational Union in 1890 that what was needed was not less but more presentation 'of the doctrines of Christ in their ethical consequences, to a far greater extent than can be recognized in the preaching of today'. The Report said that as England was 'a constitutionally-governed country, Christianity is called to be not only remedial and palliative, but constructive'. The Report was hotly debated but finally adopted.[13]

'THE WORLD AN END, AND FAITH A MEANS'

The difficulty was that many of the men most keen on the churches' involvement in political and social questions, which were ultimately the same thing, were less keen on traditional, orthodox Christian doctrine. The Revd R. J. Campbell, who eventually went over to the Church of England in a flight from what he called 'religious individualism', created a great stir with his 'New Theology' movement which spread far beyond his own Congregational Union. It started in 1907 and stressed the immanence of God. Campbell's critics said he passed through the social gospel on his way to pantheism. He did not help matters when he said that if one wanted to see the atonement at work one only needed to visit the House of Commons. Of course, that was in the happy days before the broadcasting of Parliament. (One should remember that in the general election of 1906 a Liberal Government, much beholden to Nonconformist support, had been returned. In addition, 129 Nonconformists had been elected – the largest number to date.)

As important as the 'political parsons' were the 'institutional churches' built by Congregationalists and some Baptists, and the Central Halls erected by Wesleyan Methodists. The name came from the 'institutes' attached to churches. Again, the idea did not originate with the churches but went back to the 1820s and the working-men's institutes. The new institutional churches were bold ventures, attempts to reach out to the unchurched millions by creating 'leisure centres'. They had debating societies, cycling clubs, billiard rooms, cocoa rooms, penny savings banks, burial clubs, reading rooms, gymnasiums, boys' and girls' clubs and, in at least one case, swimming baths. They were eventually surpassed by local government in our own century and even in their heyday faced stiff competition from other rivals.

Yet, the handwriting was on the wall: was the Christian religion nothing more than part of a wider social effort, something that needed buttressing and supplementing by 'leisure activities'? What would happen if tastes changed or the competition grew too stiff: might the Christian baby follow his leisurely bath-water? Would too great an emphasis on political involvement and social concern swamp the churches? A critic warned: 'The men whom the churches care to hear . . . are the men who speak most loudly upon the current political topics, and who . . . "play to the gallery" and, echoing the gallery's political watchwords, rouse the gallery to re-echo them in its turn.'[14] The veteran Baptist minister, Alexander McLaren, used the language of Scripture and metaphor when he warned: 'Martha has it all her own way now.' 'We are in danger of building so many mills and factories on the river's bank . . . that the stream will be all used up and its bed dry.'[15] Hensley Henson, later a controversial Bishop of Durham, looked at Nonconformity's apparent strength in a pamphlet entitled *Cui Bono?* Whose good? Nonconformists' 'strength and . . . weakness', he wrote, 'lie in the fact that they tend to reflect contemporary social and political movements.'[16] The dilemma was obvious: what had started out as Christian politics had become politicized Christianity. The would-be reformer had lingered too long in the house of ill fame and had succumbed to its many attractions.

In *The Screwtape Letters*, C. S. Lewis analysed this phenomenon. He has Screwtape telling Wormwood that 'What we want, if men

159

become Christians at all, is to keep them in the state of mind I call "Christianity And".' Screwtape then goes on to describe what he means:

> You know – Christianity and the Crisis, Christianity and the New Psychology, Christianity and the New Order, Christianity and Faith Healing, Christianity and Psychical Research, Christianity and Vegetarianism, Christianity and Spelling Reform . . . work on their horror of the Same Old Thing. The horror of the Same Old Thing is one of the most valuable passions we have produced in the human heart – an endless source of heresies . . .

Earlier, Screwtape advised his nephew to get his man involved in a 'cause' which demands enthusiasm. 'Then', said Screwtape,

> quietly and gradually nurse him on to the stage at which the religion becomes merely part of the 'cause', in which Christianity is valued chiefly because of the excellent arguments it can produce . . . Once you have made the World an end, and faith a means, you have almost won your man . . .[17]

POLITICS AND MORAL RECTITUDE

The importance of this to the Church's secularization under the banner of progress is the Nonconformists' legacy. Their involvement in political and social causes, which has only increased with time, has shown that the gap between religion on the periphery and politics at the centre of 'secular society' can be bridged on society's terms. Ironically, the forces of progress which created this very secular society also raised Nonconformity to its height.

This legacy has another aspect. Nonconformity's uniting of political commitment and moralistic attitudes has left behind that strong sense of moral rectitude which marks those who wish to reform, or at least change, society in this country. With the decline of the Liberal Party in the 1920s this strong 'moral sense' passed over to the Labour Party. It is not surprising that traditionally members of the Labour Party have had so little in common with their European friends of the socialist left. They simply did not speak the same language. It is interesting to note here a statement by Stanley Baldwin, the Prime Minister, in 1926. He was talking about the House of Commons: 'I find there, especially among the Labour Party, many men who fifty years ago would inevitably have gone into the Christian ministry. They have been drawn into political life from a deep desire to help the people.'[18]

This strong moral sense has affected all aspects of our national life. Opposition in England is seen to be a moral necessity among people who have inherited the Nonconformist legacy without even knowing it. In what other country do people agonize over whether or not to buy an orange because of its place of birth? Where else do people plan their holidays according to whether or not they can approve the country's system of government? This strong moral sense also sometimes produces what it produced in the nineteenth century: this is that heavy smugness and self-righteousness which admits that it is not impossible for Tory colonels to enter the Kingdom of Righteousness, but insists that it is very difficult, being somehow akin to camels and the eyes of needles. It is, therefore, hardly surprising that political movements win converts among committed churchgoers when they put forward their programmes heavily laden with moralistic language. The Campaign for Nuclear Disarmament, in one of its periodic revivals, has done just this. I recall a poster attacking the stationing of Cruise missiles in Great Britain. The poster shows Christ on his way to Golgotha. But he carries not a cross but a Cruise missile on his back. It is, of course, a misplaced metaphor because the metaphor distracts, rather than illustrates, the message. It borders on the blasphemous and minimizes the crucifixion. It reminds one, finally, of another famous misplaced metaphor, that of the American presidential candidate, William Jennings Bryan, in 1896. As the Democratic Party's candidate he attacked the gold standard and said 'you shall not crucify mankind on a cross of gold'. Mr Bryan was defeated, even if his oratory lives on.

The most important aspect of the Nonconformist legacy is this: Anglicans have never really found it difficult to move into 'opposition politics', that bewitching land where the religion of the incarnation joins hands with the secular society's concern for 'problems', the problem of peace, of poverty, of race relations, of the Common Market and on and on. The Church is seen to give a moral gloss, to be justifying herself by her concern for other questions than 'just religion'. Likewise, in politics Christians have been able to support and work for any of the major British political parties. It is worthwhile remembering that in the years after the First World War, when political parties were undergoing major changes, many prominent people argued for a 'Christian Party'. Such arguments never got off the ground because Christian morality permeated all the parties. This may all change, of course: the Labour Party appears to fall more and more under the aegis of non-Christian ideology and some bishops appear to say that Christians would have difficulty in supporting the Conservative Party.

In our own day the Church of England, and increasingly the Roman Catholic Church, have followed the lead set by the Nonconformist or Free Church denominations. The Church of England now has its 'General Synod' which, to the delight of all activists, meets three times a year. Synodical government of the Church assumes, of course, that the Church needs to be 'governed'. It is an attempt to solve the dilemma brought about by the Church's assignment to the periphery of a secular society while still being under control of a Parliament only periodically Christian. Ecclesiastical self-government in the democratic mould, with lots of elections, committees, reports, debates and discussions is acceptable to the secular world. It may, however, only confirm the Church of England's peripheral existence. On 21 July 1984 *The Times* published a letter from the Bishop of Peterborough. In it the Bishop stated his case against synodical 'government', itself a by-product of secularization:

> I left the General Synod at York last week with a sense of relief and thankfulness that never in my life shall I have to attend a synod again . . . The Synod suffers from that conceit which corrupts conscience. Some of its members imagine that the Synod owns the dioceses and parishes of England . . . It feeds itself, like a parasite, on the parishes, who, willy nilly, pay for it; and it has produced a new sort of ecclesiastical politician, whose only salvation is that it should swiftly be made both sadder and wiser.

The same criticisms could be made against the other Parliament sitting in Westminster.

It is one of the saddest ironies of the present day that where the Christian Church is most restricted in her freedom to speak, her influence carries greatest weight. But in those countries where she is freest to speak, western Europe, Britain or the United States, her pronouncements carry little weight at all if they go against current trends of thought: her wide freedom to speak seems based on the fact that no one will listen. In the United States the strength of the Protestant Fundamentalists and the Roman Catholic-based 'Pro-Life' movement should not blind us to the fact that constitutionally the United States are a secular society. For many years there was an unwritten understanding that America was a Christian country. But recently, in three decisions (Engel v. Vitale, Abington Township School District v. Schempp and Murray v. Curlett), the Supreme Court outlawed Bible reading, nondenominational prayers and the Lord's Prayer in state schools.

THE PRICE TO BE PAID

Now, to talk of the Church's 'de-secularization' we must understand how it became secularized. This was a long process which began with the gradual destruction of the old alliance between Church and realm. This was destroyed in the nineteenth century under the banner of Progress. Originally the devotion to Progress was based on undeniable national success in coping with rapid and tremendous changes. In time, however, Progress could stand on its own two feet and needed no justification in fact. Because of the changes in society the old values fell away and were replaced by a new creed, the belief in individualism, of inevitable improvement, of self-fulfilment and happiness above all else. Inevitably Nonconformist denominations did best in such a world because of their traditional emphasis on personal salvation, the priesthood of all believers and a dislike of the Church of England's establishment, itself an abiding symbol of the old order.

Increasingly, however, this new society developed its own momentum. Churches were pushed to the periphery of society. The Church of England, no longer a vital aspect of the national constitution, joined the others and became *primus inter pares*. Politics – the belief that parliamentary action could solve all problems, of which there were increasingly so many – became the new religion of the nation. After all, had not parliamentary government led the nation's successful struggle to combine vast changes with traditional respect for social order?

The Churches could either resign themselves to a concern 'only with religion' or they could adopt the new currency of politics as their own. Inevitably, Nonconformity became most heavily involved in political/ social questions. The price they have had to pay has been a heavy one. Nonconformity's decline is due to many factors which are far too complex to go into here. But one cause stands out: secularization. When Professor David Martin examined the returns of the Bible Society's 1979 religious survey he divided the Free Churches into two groups. The first he labelled Evangelical (Baptists, Pentecostals and Independents); the second he called Liberal (Methodists and URC). It is the 'liberal' denominations that have suffered and are continuing to suffer the greatest decline in adherents. The URC, the child of Congregationalism, that most political of the Old Dissent, is the leader in political Christianity. It declines fastest of all. The 'Evangelical' denominations eschew politics for the gospel and they either decline least of all or, in some cases, grow. Dr Martin's explanation for the Liberal decline is this:[19]

> Both [Methodists and URC] are liberal and therefore have an open door towards the wider community. In a relatively secular situation their young people more easily walk out through the door rather than bring their compeers in. Patterns of adolescent association are more and more with those who are not members of their own denomination. Being open they are not oriented to forcing their own religious attachments on those with whom they associate.

Many groups find themselves in a vicious cycle: the more figures fall the more do they involve themselves in politics; the more they do this the more the figures fall and on and on.

Again, secularization continues apace. In 1984 there were calls for alteration to the Religious Educaion given in state schools to make it less 'Christian'. The old dream of a 'nondenominational' but still Christian society, based on the schools' syllabus, has become a bogy to the descendants of those Nonconformists who saw it as the way forward. In America, as we have seen, 'nondenominational Christianity' in the schools has been virtually destroyed by the courts. Indeed, in recent years America has seen the development of specifically 'Christian schools' by people, such as the Southern Baptists, who had always been the staunchest supporters of the state system. In England last year there was a recommendation that the oath in court should be abolished. The oath is, of course, like all oaths, an appeal to God to witness that what one says is true. It is a pact between man and God, not man and the court. The 'reformers' obviously feel that God has no place in an English courtroom. It is what John Keble called 'throwing off the restraint'.

Despite the advancing tide of secularization, the Church of England remains established, a reminder that full 'pluralism' has yet to be achieved. There are still periodic and symbolic reminders of the old ties between God and England – in the Coronation, the Queen's Silver Jubilee services, the Royal Wedding of 1981. All of these, of course, centre on the monarchy for the monarchy is the only part of parliamentary government that remains wholly Christian. Indeed, the Church itself could learn something from the monarchy.

FACING THE FUTURE

Although the Sovereign today remains as indispensable a part of Parliament as ever, her role in the day-to-day conduct of government, while more important than many journalists might imagine, is no longer crucial. The momentum has long since passed to other places. Yet, the Sovereign's importance in British life is greater than it has ever been. This is due partially to the Crown's 'staying power'. Governments come and governments go, some more happily than others; but it is the Crown that remains, the embodiment of lasting virtues, of national character and history. The occasional public displays of the majesty of the Crown, as in the State Opening of Parliament, are timely reminders of this abiding truth of the Constitution. The Queen's constitutional position is enhanced by her own character and her fame for hard work, dedication, knowledge and great store of common sense. She has far more in common with her subjects than her ministers often have. But her influence is also due to a large degree to the fact that the Crown has learned to provide a leadership and an influence apart from politics. The Queen's Christmas Broadcast often gives a clearer and more understandable presentation of the Christian Gospel than do many bishops. In charity work, the role of the family, education, the arts and conversation the Crown gives a valuable lead.

The Church can learn from this. If the Church of England no longer holds the position she did in the past, she still has an envied position in national life. She does nothing to enhance this by an obsession with political questions in which she becomes hopelessly entangled with party politics. She gains when she takes clear and firm stands on moral questions in which she has authority to speak. The Church of England will always find herself in a difficult position. The provinces of Canterbury and York were never designed to stand on their own, cut off from the rest of the Western Church. The Reformation left the Church in England isolated. The Crown stepped in to shore up the weakened structure, like a terraced house that has lost its neighbours to make room for a new road. Now that alliance is a thing of the past. The Christian society that both the sixteenth-century Reformation and the seventeenth-century Restoration settlements assumed seems to be crumbling.

The most recent example of the Church's ultimately futile attempt to move from the periphery back into the centre of secular society is the demand for the ordination of women to the priesthood and the episcopate. This campaign is essentially a product of secular society and the 'women's rights' movement of the last hundred years. While the objections to the ordination of women to the priesthood are theological, the arguments for are secular in essence. They are based on a demand that once again the Church show herself worthy of her society by fully adopting society's rules, in this case the demand for 'equality' by the self-appointed spokespersons for 'women'. Our secular world has always hated any relic of the old 'exclusive system' left over from the past. An all-male priesthood is just such a 'relic' and as such must be removed.

The national worship of inevitable progress in all things is dead. To many people, 'progress' is a dirty word and implies disregard for our environment or a manipulation of innocent people. The grandchildren of those devoted to Progress are often today devoted to 'protection' and to maintaining the unspoilt villages in which they live and from which they pronounce on the country's problems. But the ghost of Progress still haunts those liberal intellectuals terrified of the 'same old thing'. It haunts many an episcopal palace with bishops, in Sir Robert Peel's delightful phrase, 'ever on the fret' to make a stir.

The Church of England stands on the periphery and looks longingly at the centre whence she has been pushed. Many of the Free Churches dissipate their witness in vain attempts to reach the secular centre. The Roman Catholics are not quite sure what to do: the glitter of power attracts them and the glamour of the British Council of Churches is powerful among all religious activists, Catholics included. But the Churches will never regain the centre and all the struggles to do so will be in vain. They can never keep up with the 'impatient patrons of innovations', as John Keble wisely called them. So far as the Church of England is concerned, she can play the role God has assigned her in English life in so far as she is prepared to remain loyal to the reality of human nature and God's salvation delivered once and for all in Christ. Her resumption of the duties history has laid upon her will never be along the futile path of secular appeasement: if our history shows us nothing else, it shows us this.

NOTES

1   The Revd William Cuff, Presidential Address, 23 April 1900, *Baptist Union Handbook for 1901* (London 1901), pp. 96, 97.

2   John Cudlip to Miss Annette Christie, 2 May 1915, in the Revd Andrew Clark, 'Echoes of the Great War', manuscript diary in the Bodleian Library, Oxford, MSS. Eng. Hist. e 107ff. 105v–114v.

3   Jacob Burckhardt to Friedrich von Preen, 25 September 1890 in Alexander Dru (ed. and trans.), *The Letters of Jacob Burckhardt* (New York n.d.), p. 222.

4   *John Cassell's Illustrated History of England* (eds. J. F. Smith and William Howitt), (London 1857), pp. iii–iv, 600.

5   David Martin, 'Age and Sex Variations of Church Attenders' in *Prospects for the Eighties* (London 1980), p. 14.

6   This ancient constitution was reflected in the Prayer Book in the five 'annexed' services. The services were (1) the accession of the reigning sovereign; (2) the commemoration of the Gunpowder Plot (5 November); (3) the martyrdom of King Charles I (30 January); (4) the restoration of the monarchy (29 May); (5) the landing of the Prince of Orange (4 November). They were removed by a Royal Warrant of 1859 and new forms of services for Accession Day were ordered. This was another blow to the alliance of Church and realm in which both shared a common heritage which both had created.

7   Cf. Canon Henry Lewis, *Modern Rationalism as seen at Work in its Biographies* (London 1913), pp. 88, 94.

8   John Stuart Mill, *On Liberty* (Everyman edn, 1968), pp. 65, 152, 150, 138. (First published in 1859.)

9   Canon Samuel A. Barnett, *Religion and Politics Lectures Given in Westminster Abbey* (London 1911), p. 3.

10 Matthew Arnold, *Culture and Anarchy: An Essay in Political and Social Criticism* (The Nelson Library n.d.) p. 141. (First published in 1869.)

11 *Northamptonshire Nonconformist*, November 1891.

12 J. Carvell Williams, MP, Chairman's Address, 7 May 1900, *Congregational Union Year Book for 1901.* (London 1901), p. 30.

13 *Congregational Union Year Book for 1891* (London 1891), pp. 32–6.

14 'A Nonconformist Minister', *Nonconformity and Politics* (London 1909), p. 137.

15 The Revd Alexander McLaren, Presidential Address, 7 October 1901, *Baptist Union Handbook for 1902* (London 1902), pp. 124–5.

16 *Cui Bono?* (London, 5th edn 1899), p. 17.

17 C. S. Lewis, *The Screwtape Letters* (London 1942), pp. 126, 42–3.

18 Stanley Baldwin, *On England, and Other Addresses* (London 1926), p. 196.

19 David Martin, 'Age and Sex Variations of Church Attenders' in *Prospects for the Eighties*, p. 14.

5 Desecularizing the Social Gospel

GRAHAM LEONARD

In his introduction to this book, William Oddie quotes these words from a sermon of John Henry Newman: '. . . And hence it is right that many pursuits, in themselves honest and right, are nevertheless to be engaged in with caution, lest they seduce us; and those perhaps with special caution, which tend to the well-being of men in this life. The sciences, for instance, of good government, acquiring wealth, of preventing and relieving want, and the like, are for this reason especially dangerous; for fixing, as they do, our exertions on this world as an end, they go far to persuade us that they have no other end . . .'[1]

ESTABLISHING THE PRIORITIES

The fact that these concerns, and the actions which implement them, involve danger and are to be approached with caution gives no warrant to Christians to shrink from them or to eschew them as being in some way incompatible with Christian discipleship. Our Lord's words, as reported in the Gospels, have a full-blooded ring about them and there is nothing in them of the nicely-calculated more or less. His sayings about taking up the cross, putting our hands to the plough and not turning back, and cutting off our limbs if they will cause us to stumble, are not those of a cautious person seeking to avoid danger by the exercise of moderation. Yet he does tell us to be wise as serpents and repeatedly warns us of the danger of being deflected from our primary objective by a devotion to secondary ends. Business concerns, even the demands of family life and the filial duty of burying one's parents, have to be subordinated to seek the Kingdom of God and attend the divine banquet (Luke 14). Nowhere does our Lord suggest that the former concerns are of no account such as to justify our neglect of them. On the contrary, it is precisely because they are of such importance and demand our attention and concern, that there is danger of our

169

allowing them a priority which they cannot properly claim. Newman himself laid great emphasis upon the authority of conscience. Because he saw it as operating in every sphere of human life, and recognized the danger of its identification with self-will, he was acutely aware of the need to examine the motives underlying concern for temporal matters.

THE GOSPEL IS SOCIAL

The need to listen to Newman's warning is most urgent in the realm of politics, and particularly so at the present time in view of the understanding of the nature and purpose of politics which has come to predominate. The cry to 'keep politics out of religion' usually arises not out of an *a priori* belief that politics and religion can and should never mix but out of a false understanding of its nature and purpose which in turn leads to undesirable characteristics in its practice. The Christian gospel is above all concerned with 'the taking of our manhood into God', and the word manhood embraces every aspect of human life, including the life of society. What is unacceptable is the attitude which reverses the process and which sees religion as no more than an adjunct which we can pray in aid of our desire to ameliorate man and society. It is this attitude which has come to be associated with the term 'social gospel' in its pejorative sense. It must be emphasized that to be critical of it in that sense is not to imply that the gospel is not social. It is set within the context given by the Old Testament in which the life of the individual is essentially and inextricably bound up with the life of the community and its social and political life. Further, in the New Testament redemption is corporate by virtue of incorporation into the Body of Christ, the New Israel, in which both man and creation are redeemed. The idea of a purely individual salvation is alien to the New Testament. As in the Old Testament, personal responsibility is to be exercised in the light of membership of the Body.

Both for the Church as an institution and for individuals, the exercise of that responsibility requires an involvement in the political sphere whether active or passive. The attitude of both will depend upon the basis upon which the particular political system operates and the purpose which it is intended to achieve. Neither the Church nor individual Christians should endorse a political system which is based upon an understanding of and an approach to politics which are

170

fundamentally opposed to Christian belief about God, man and reality. This point was made in the Report 'The Church of England and Politics – Reflections on Christian Social Engagement' presented by the Board for Social Responsibility in 1980.[2] The Report took the form of a personal statement by the then Secretary, Mr. Giles Ecclestone, who wrote as follows (para. 18):

> Those Christians who ask anxiously about the Church's involvement in politics may be reflecting a debased view of politics. It is possible to go to the other extreme and take the view that 'politics is all', that the reality to which the Gospel and the Christian faith obscurely refer is specifically and solely the public world of human society, its possibilities, needs and dilemmas. This view, expressed originally by Feuerbach and Marx in the context of their social criticism of religion, is integral to the understanding of Christian faith in 'political theology' and in certain of the theologians of liberation. It reflects the attempt to cast in coherent form the deep ethical concern which is a feature of biblical religion and which finds expression today, in Churches throughout the world, in challenges to economic, social and racial injustice. But the effect of the particular analysis adopted (like many politically conservative interpretations of the Christian faith before it) is to make Christian faith – and not merely Christian theology – subservient to the achievement of specific political goals. As such it becomes an ideology (in Marx's terms), a set of ideas which may contribute to a desired end but say nothing true about the nature or reality.

Giles Ecclestone himself writes of the dangers of abstract intellectual reflections concerning the Church's engagement in politics: 'The more comprehensive the intellectual system the more it will lead people to ignore or undervalue events and realities which do not fit.'[3] But for the reason expressed in the quotation above, he recognizes the need for the Church to look deeply at the rationale of its political involvement and to seek to understand what is going on in society as well as engage in action over specific issues.

WHAT IS POLITICS?

The first question which has to be asked is 'What is politics?' Since the

Age of the Enlightenment in the eighteenth century, the answers to that question will almost invariably reflect one of two basic positions. The first group of answers will be based upon the view which sees politics as the means by which a particular ideology is propagated and implemented with the intention of bringing about human happiness. This view has its origins in the eighteenth century in the fundamental shift which took place, when, to put it very crudely, one framework of thought, in which man saw himself as responsible to God for his existence and the management of his affairs, was replaced by a framework of thought, in which man saw himself potentially as the master of all things. Much has been written about the reasons which led to this change. The translation of Arabic writings into Latin, the impact of Aristotelian philosophy, the achievements of the Renaissance, which was essentially anthropocentric, and the development of Newtonian physics all contributed to make an explosive mixture which led to the change. Three characteristics of its nature are particularly important. First, it embodied an extraordinarily optimistic view of human nature as capable of infinite progress by the mastery of nature. As Bishop Lesslie Newbigin has written:

> By the end of the [eighteenth] century the leading thinkers in western Europe were convinced that a light had indeed dawned compared with which the preceding centuries of European history and the previous history of most of the human race were darkness. Whatever might have been the achievements of the Greeks and the Chinese, they had not progressed. Modern Europe has surpassed them all.[4a]

So much was this so that

> Condorcet, the most luminous exponent of the neo-Rousseauian ideas of the French Revolution went so far in his predictions of human progress as almost to presage the abolition of human mortality by science.[4b]

Secondly, the possibility of 'explaining' many natural processes which had hitherto remained mysteries, led to an identification of 'explanations' with absolute truth and thereby provided a framework for the mastery of nature by man. Thirdly, it had the effect of replacing a society in which men thought of their duties with a society in which they thought of their rights.

In the realm of politics these ideas were developed by Rousseau. For him, there was a deep inner conflict between the individual in his loneliness and the individual in the life of the community. He spoke of the irreconcilable contradiction between 'our duties and our inclinations, between nature and the social institutions, between man and citizen', and he saw the possibility of happiness only in the destruction of the one or the other, of the man or the citizen. He opted for the former (though the conflict remained within himself). In so doing, he ruled out the Christian religion which he regarded as essentially individual-istic, so much so that he could say that 'a society of true Christians would no longer be a society of men', believing as he did that it was wholly 'opposed to the social spirit'.

So Professor Ionescu can write:

> Poor Rousseau had done the harm. Like the sorcerer's apprentice he had uncorked one of the most intoxicating ideas in the whole history of ideas – that people can be made happy by politics, while politics can be made by the people. That idea, once out of the bottle, expanded like a gas, penetrating human minds from within and from without, detonating a series of consecutive explosions which have rumbled from the eighteenth to the twentieth century. Gradually it replaced the old doctrine of salvation and became what Jacques Ellul rightly called a political soteriology.[5]

IDEOLOGY AND PRAGMATISM

With his concept of the *volonté générale*, which was taken as identifying the right and the good with the will of the majority, the way was open for the growth of ideological politics, the characteristics of which can be summarized as follows:

1 The role of politics is to provide human happiness, understood in material terms.
2 It is based on an ideology, which is justified on the grounds that it is the will of the majority or of the ruling party.
3 The use of political power to enforce human happiness, so conceived, is justified on the grounds (a) that it is the role of politics to provide happiness and (b) that politics has the right in what it is and how it is to be achieved.

173

4 Men and women are judged to be capable of being made happy by political action.

5 Politics is essentially the provision of human rights provided that such rights are compatible with the requirements of what the ideology believes to be necessary for corporate human happiness.

6 Politics is regarded as autonomous and as having no responsibility to moral absolutes outside itself.

The approach of ideological politics is beautifully summed up in the words of T. S. Eliot when he speaks of those who

> . . . constantly try to escape
> From the darkness outside and within
> By dreaming of systems so perfect
> that no one will need to be good.[6]

The second group of answers to the question 'What is the purpose of politics?' reflect a pragmatic view. Professor Ghitu Ionescu in his book *Politics and the Pursuit of Happiness* adopts the following definition of politics:

> the regulation of the co-existence of human beings within a unit of rule, with a view to improving it in the present and in the future. It is assumed that the improvement depends on the extent to which the regulation is guided by the observance of laws; and on how much it reduces the part coercion plays, and hence increases the part which participation plays, in that lawful regulation.

By way of comment on his definition, Professor Ionescu first draws attention to the fact that it speaks of co-existence of human beings, that is, living men and women who are mortal and who, once they are dead, are physically cut off from the enmeshment of regulating activities which is the ambit of politics. He justifies what he calls 'this extraordinary platitude' by the fact that the missing factor in modern political science is precisely the mortality of man.

> The units of conceptualization and of statistical qualification are abstract and permanent categories or prototypes called men, Frenchmen, Americans, citizens, voters, workers, women, blacks, urban and rural dwellers, etc. . . . But the specific

individual man, who is meant to be the object of the social science dies, or as Unanumo would insist, *'above all* – dies'.

It is within this death-bound time that real human beings must regulate their ephemeral coexistence. Nothing that mortal men regulate in their public life can attain finality.[7]

Professor Ionescu then points out that whereas the House of Commons recognizes that its sovereign decisions cannot bind future Parliaments, the French and Russian Revolutions aimed at Utopia, and, he adds, their failures have only served to lead to the rediscovery of the tragic sense of politics by modern man.

He continues to comment on his definition as follows:

Hence the choice of the expression 'to regulate' in defining politics as the regulation of the coexistence of human beings. The expression 'to regulate' was chosen with two considerations in mind. On the one hand 'to regulate' is used in preference to the phrase 'to solve'. For politics . . . never solves the problems facing the community. The community itself is after all in a constant state of intragenerational transition, and the problems change so constantly that they can never be really comprehended, in the double sense of the word. New human beings face new problems or the same problems in the same context. They can only regulate them for the time being. On the other hand, the problems of human coexistence produce conflicts between different rights, obligations and above all between the points of view of different categories of people living together. The use of a neutral expression like 'to regulate' implies that the ultimate decision can be taken by different means and by different procedures, ranging from persuasion to participation.[8]

When giving his definition, Professor Ionescu said that he assumed that the improvement brought about by the regulation of coexistence depended on the extent to which the regulation is guided by the observance of laws, and he develops this statement as follows:

Different kinds of 'regulation' are necessary in order to establish the coexistence of human beings. The regulation of relations between individuals is achieved by civil customs and laws. Relations between the individual and the community as a whole, of which he is a member by 'association' or 'contract', or with the institutions of that community, are regulated by public or constitutional laws.

The laws themselves whose role is to prescribe the regulations and to indicate how they should be made to work, are made by the individuals of the community, or by the community of individuals; and yet the laws also originate from some supreme, ancestral and unwritten Laws, Commandments, Customs or Virtues, which correspond also to the permanent aspiration to the good which is engraved in the conscience of human beings from their mysterious origin. Conscience, Virtue, Law, Right and Justice are as closely linked together in the moral field as Religion, Ethics and Politics are in the interdisciplinary field.[9]

Professor Ionescu's criticism of ideological politics springs from his understanding of the nature of man and of society. In the book from which I have quoted, he also criticizes it as being incompatible with the essentially functional industrial society. He draws attention to the fact that the epistemological change in the eighteenth century produced 'the antagonistic twins', namely functional industrial society and ideological politics and that since the beginning of the twentieth century the latter has become increasingly inadequate as a means of regulating the coexistence of human beings in an industrial society, and hence they have become dysfunctional. The approach of ideological politics is not confined to avowedly ideological régimes, as in Russia or Iran. It has penetrated all political thinking and Professor Ionescu believes it to be a likely explanation of the present crisis of political credulity in all industrial societies, capitalist and socialist alike. In this country, it is frequently assumed by those who are critical of the involvement of the Church in politics that those who are involved are invariably left-wing. To some extent that is true here but is certainly not universal. There is, for example, in the USA a very right-wing religious involvement in politics as well as one of the left.

POLITICS AND SCIENTIFIC METHOD

The second group of answers to the question 'What is the purpose of politics?' will include the approach of Sir Karl Popper, whose social and political ideas spring from his epistemology and his understanding of scientific method. It is for this reason that it is first necessary to say something about the latter.

The traditional view of scientific method is, to put it very crudely, that you assemble facts, you produce a theory, which then provides you with objective knowledge. Popper criticized this view mainly on two grounds. First, he maintained that facts do not in themselves create their own meaning. He used to say to his students; 'Go and observe.' They would respond by asking him what they should observe, because no one just observes. There is an element of selection in any act of observation which derives from a purpose, an intuition or a theory. Facts do not create their own meaning, nor impose it upon us.

Secondly, he pointed out that the empirical observation of facts can never give us absolute, objective truth. One classic example he used was the statement, 'All swans are white'. However many white swans have been observed it still does not prove that statement to be true. The probability that all swans are white may be very high but there is always the possibility that a black swan will be seen. In other words, the statement can be falsified but it cannot be verified. He also points out that you can make scientific statements which are difficult to falsify but give very little information. For example, the statement, 'It is usually raining somewhere', is very difficult to falsify but it says very little. It is a low-information statement, it has a high degree of probability and it is virtually unfalsifiable, whereas other statements can have a high information content, be easily falsifiable and have a low degree of probability.

Popper, in other words, says that human beings exist in a relationship to reality, which continually confronts them, which they seek to explain and which creates problems. As a result, theories and hypotheses are created, some of which are falsifiable, some not. They are all attempts to construct in the mind of man expressions of the reality in which he lives and by which he seeks to regulate his life and make sense of it. What is relevant to the particular discussions is his insistence that just as no scientific theory can be said to be absolutely true, so no ideology can be regarded as embodying absolute truths or as acquiring absolute authority, which justifies its application at all costs. Hence Popper stands for the Open Society in which politics is seen as a way of problem-solving and is not used as the means of enforcing an ideology.

177

Two points need to be made by way of comment on Popper's position. First, he rejected the position of the logical positivists who made a distinction between statements which were empirically verifiable and which made sense and those which could not be so verified and were regarded as making no sense. For Popper the distinction is between scientific statements which are capable of being falsified and non-scientific statements which are not but which are also capable of expressing the truth about reality. It was for this reason among others that Popper is so critical of the word 'scientific' being applied to the theories of Marx.

Secondly, the fact that human beings cannot express the nature and meaning of reality with absolute certainty, does not deny the existence of reality. Indeed, it may be said that Popper's philosophy and method depends upon the encounters which man experiences with reality. This point will be seen to be important when the relationship of revelation to ideology is concerned.

ELECTIVE DICTATORSHIP AND FREEDOM UNDER LAW

Lord Hailsham, in his book *The Dilemma of Democracy* also makes the distinction between the two understandings of the purpose of politics, when he refers to the 'two inconsistent opinions about the nature of democracy', and suggests that the politics of the next twenty-five years may well depend upon the encounter between the two, and that more will depend upon the outcome than the future of the British Isles.

> The two theories are the theory of centralized democracy, known as elective dictatorship, and the theory of limited government, in any language the doctrine of freedom under law.
>
> Between the two theories there can ultimately be no compromise. Both may depend upon universal adult suffrage. But the one will assert the right of a bare majority in a single chamber assembly, possibly elected on a first-past-the-post basis, to assert its will over a whole people whatever that will may be. It will end in a rigid economic plan and, I believe, in a siege economy, a curbed and subservient judiciary and a regulated press. It will impose uniformity on the whole nation in the interest of what it claims to be social justice. It will insist on equality. It will distrust all

forms of eccentricity and distinction. It will crush local autonomy. It will dictate the structure, form and content of education. It may tolerate but will certainly do its best to corrupt or destroy, religion.

Lord Hailsham points out that centralized democracy is not the prerogative of Socialism or of left-wing extremists, but can equally well be an expression of Fascism and the right-wing.

The alternative to it is based on:

> the old doctrine inherent from the very first, that is from the time of Bracton onwards, in English law, that those in a position of political authority may not rule absolutely, that, being human, even kings may not place themselves above the law and may not make laws which affront the instructed conscience of the commonalty . . .

and it offers precisely what centralized democracy denies.

> In place of uniformity it offers diversity. In place of equality it offers justice. In place of the common good, it protects the rights of minorities and the individual. As an alternative to regulation it propounds the rule of law. It does not seek to overthrow governments or institutions, or abolish universal franchise or popular rule. And it prescribes limits beyond which governments and Parliaments must not go and it suggests means by which they can be compelled to observe those limits. In place of concentration it diffuses power . . .[10]

It is unfair and unwarranted to suppose that those who advocate centralized democracy or ideological politics do so out of a desire to exercise power in an improper way. Both the French and the Russian Revolution sprang from a passionate concern to oppose unjust and oppressive régimes. Marx was moved originally to develop his political philosophy by the plight of the oppressed and deprived. Nor must it be supposed that those who are committed to the Open Society and to a more pragmatic view of politics are callous or indifferent towards miserable and unjust human conditions. As with all human activities, both can be corrupted, the one by excessive claims for the autonomy of politics and its capacity to effect change, leading to a denial of the very liberties which it is intended to recover; the other by a too-ready

179

acquiescence in the *status quo* leading to the condoning of evils which can and should be remedied.

DEMOCRACY AND THE NATURE OF THE GOSPEL

The real question, however, is not whether the one is more liable to corruption than the other but whether either is based upon fundamental assumptions which are incompatible with the true nature of man and therefore with the Christian gospel. It is the argument of this chapter that the ideological approach is so incompatible and that whenever Christian social concern and action is inspired or affected by it, it is secularized in the sense that its basis is incompatible with the gospel. The term 'secularization' is sometimes used in the context of ideological politics to mean that what is wrong is the substitution of another ideology for a Christian one. This is a superficial and dangerous notion. Any ideology, even the Christian one, produces undesirable effects if it is made the basis of autonomous political policy and action. To some, this may seem strange, possibly even to question commitment to the truth of the gospel. A Christian who advocates the pragmatic view of politics may well be charged with being lukewarm and not having the courage of his convictions. But the very nature of the gospel requires the acceptance of certain basic truths about the nature of God, his dealings with man, and the nature of man which preclude the ideological approach.

Before considering these truths, it is perhaps necessary to emphasize that orthodox Christian belief has always been regarded as recognizing and fulfilling true human nature, not imposing upon it an interpretation or requirements alien to it. This springs from the fact that the God whom Christians know and love in Christ is God the Creator whose purposes for men are realized in Christ by the fulfilment of human nature.

REVELATION AND SOCIETY

A few years ago the author of this chapter was asked to contribute to a series of articles under the title 'Is Christianity Credible?'[11] He pointed out that it was not possible simply to argue from the authority of traditional Christian beliefs based on the gospel. To have done so would have meant arguing in a circle. The truth of the very belief in question would have to be assumed. The credibility of Christian doctrine lies in the fact that it accepts, redeems and fulfils the fundamental characteristics of human beings and does so in a way which enables man to live with his paradoxes rather than attempt to remove them by denying one or the other aspect of them. The problems of time and eternity, of grace and free-will, of the individual and the community, of the ambiguity of creation are not solved. But neither are they denied existence by the reduction of life to that in time alone, by emphasis on one's selfhood or on the community to the exclusion of the other, by capitulation to the physical order as wholly determinative or by a doctrine of irresistible grace, both of which reject any real element of freedom in choice or decision. In Christ we are enabled to live with these problems and make sense of them in terms of the eternal purpose of God and the eternal destiny of man.

What, then, are the basic reasons which lead a Christian to support a pragmatic view of politics and to regard any understanding of the social gospel which is based on an ideological approach as secularization of that gospel? The first reason derives from the nature of Christianity as a revealed religion. Revelation is the self-communication of God which is mediated through his acts in creation and in Christ. These acts provide the raw material upon which the Church reflects and by which it lives as it seeks to understand their meaning and appreciate their significance. The record of those acts is contained in the Holy Scriptures and their significance in its most basic form is contained in the Creeds, which have the authority of acceptance by the mind of the Church throughout the ages. But each successive generation has to seek to understand and apply that revelation for its time. Revelation is closed only in the sense that Christ, who is the fullness of the revelation of God, has been and is already present in history. Revelation continues in the sense that God is the living Christ through the Spirit, who reveals the meaning of his acts to us throughout history and does so in a way which is consonant with and certainly does not contradict the self-communication which occurred in the incarnate life of Christ. This continued acceptance and understanding of revelation is undertaken by the Church on earth, which is composed of human beings who, though incorporated into Christ, are sinful and imperfect. It must always live under judgement, continually testing its understanding and expression of God's revelation by the Scriptures and the creeds, recognizing that no re-expression of that revelation will be perfect.

181

This means that it cannot claim that degree of authority for a particular expression of the meaning of the Scriptures and the creeds which would justify its use as an ideology to be imposed at all cost on society, as is the case, for example, with that of Marxist-Leninism. While Christians are committed to live in obedience to that revelation, seeking to be grasped more fully and more deeply by it, they can only offer it to the world as the way of redemption and not seek to enforce it.

Secondly, the revelation of God in Christ reveals God as Love, who has created man in his own image, with the freedom to choose whether to respond to God or not. In his revelation and in redeeming acts God respects that freedom. This is supremely evident upon the cross which still allows us the freedom to choose. The cross does not compel anyone. There is no moral blackmail nor manipulation in the cross. The ultimate distinction between good and evil is made evident and man is left free to choose and to respond to God's act of supreme love in which he bears the cost. Any action which purports to be Christian but which seeks to compel men and women to be good is incompatible with the meaning of the cross. It is for this reason, among others, that Christians have set such store by conscience. Traditional moral theology is based upon two fundamental principles. The first is *conscientia semper sequenda* – conscience must always be followed; and the second is *conscientia semper reformanda* – conscience is always in need of correction. In other words, man's freedom to choose is always respected, hence the need for respect of minorities. But the conscience of an individual or a corporate body is never identified with the perfect good or the will of God. (In the case of someone who holds a position of authority in the Church, the same principles hold good. So if, say, a bishop is so far removed from the mind of the Church in doctrine or morals, that it would be a scandal for him to be allowed to continue to act in the name of the Church, he must be deprived of his position by external authority acting in its name. It must be assumed that he is acting 'in good conscience', even if it be thoroughly wrong. His conscience must be respected but he must be told that it is so distorted as to prevent him acting in the Church's name. What would be wrong would be for moral pressure to be brought to bear upon him to act contrary to his own conscience.)

FREEDOM AND DEPENDENCE

The third reason for rejecting an ideological view of politics is that it denies a fundamental characteristic of human beings, namely their dependence upon each other, their dependence upon creation, and, the Christian would add, their dependence upon God. Dependence is one of man's characteristics which he most readily rejects, believing falsely that such rejection is necessary if he is to exercise his freedom. Philosophers, such as Feuerbach, in the eighteenth century, rejected belief in God on the grounds that belief involved dependence upon God, which violated the autonomy of the individual. The plain fact is that we are dependent on one another, and upon the created world for our very existence. In the present context, the important significance of the fact is that no one and no group or élite, however intelligent, well-meaning or powerful, must seek to establish a position in which others are wholly dependent upon them. Ideological politics, by its very nature, involves such a position. It invariably leads to the dictator, the inner ring, the élite, the committee, the party which regards itself as justified in pressing its views and policies upon the masses who, for their well-being, must accept their good offices. The Open Society, limited government under the law, on the other hand recognizes the mutual dependence of people upon each other, the dependence of those who govern upon the governed to provide the resources for them to do so, and the responsibility which those who govern have for listening to and learning from those whom they govern.

The fourth reason is that one cannot, as ideological politics assumes, *make* people happy. To say that is not to be cynical. It is again to recognize a fundamental fact about human nature, the Christian understanding of man, of reflecting about it and of transcending it. The conditions in which he lives, his upbringing, his environment are of the utmost importance and require our deep attention and concern. They cannot be disregarded in favour of a purely spiritual view of man's well-being and salvation. At the same time, in themselves, they cannot make a man happy. Happiness ultimately depends upon the exercise of man's peculiar characteristic, namely, that of being able to act responsibly. In the Old Testament, the human person is first a creature of God, forced out of the clay of the ground. His existence, his bodiliness, meant not so much being an individual as sharing in a common humanity and sharing in nature as created by God. As a human person, however, he is distinguished by being responsible – to God, to his neighbours and to nature. That responsible existence is not seen as the activity of a soul seeking to control or make sense of a body which is evil or worthless. It is the activity of a whole person who shares bodily existence. In the early years of Israel's history, a man's responsibility was seen in corporate terms. His actions affected others and he shared the effects of theirs. He was affected by the attitude of the whole nation. When the recognition of personal responsibility developed, notably in the teaching of the prophet Ezekiel, the distinctiveness of the individual was seen not in his separate bodily existence, defined by the boundary of his body, but in the 'uniqueness of the Divine Word or call to every man, which demanded from him an inalienable response'. It is through the free exercise of that response that a man achieves happiness. It cannot be forced upon him in spite of it.

This is particularly true of legislation, by which political aims are given precise and concrete expression. The way legislation is understood tends to reflect one of the two approaches to politics. The ideological view tends to esteem the power of legislation far too highly and to suppose that it can change reality or make things right or wrong. Such an attitude is not confined to politicians. For example, I have heard lawyers say that to declare illegitimate children legitimate in the eyes of the law does not simply make them legitimate but actually alters the fact that at the time of their birth their parents were not married. All that a law can do is to make something legal or illegal and define penalties which will result if certain acts are done or not done. Certainly legislation can have a very profound effect in shaping attitudes, not least when it changes an existing situation. To make something legal which was illegal, is very often taken to imply that the action in question becomes right, as well as legal, and has the effect of encouraging it. But the most that legislation can do is to make it easier for people to be good and harder for them to be bad.

Ideological politics, which accepts no authority over the ideology conceived, and which, therefore, sets its own criteria of what is right and good, invariably sees legislation as a way of implementing its own values and supposes that legislation can determine the way people think. Ideological politics with its subordination of the individual to the State, does not believe that dissent has any right to exist, as it allows for no higher criteria to which the individual can rightly appeal. The achievement of happiness is ultimately dependent upon the exercise of that inner freedom to which ideological politics by its very nature denies expression.

THE MORAL TYRANNY OF IDEOLOGICAL POLITICS

The exercise of human freedom depends upon the recognition of moral absolutes to which both individuals and corporate bodies, whether governed or governing, are subject and to which they can appeal. The traditional understanding of democracy in the West has accepted that there are certain laws which are permanent and of universal validity, under which all stand in judgement. These laws are God-given and reflect the nature of man and society as created by God. They are not made by men though men have the responsibility of implementing them in the context of the society into which they have been born and which they have a responsibility to help to create for the future. The recognition and acceptance of moral absolutes involves accepting the limitations of human wisdom and of political power. The authority which is properly given to a moral absolute cannot be given to any one particular way devised by man of seeking to implement it. The failure to appreciate the point has led to great confusion and serious misunderstanding as this writer can illustrate from an experience of his own. In an address on 'The Christian in Politics', he drew attention to the strange fact that whereas in the case of fundamental Christian doctrines, such as the divinity of Christ, it seemed that nowadays any view was acceptable, when it came to political policies to deal with the evils of society, one particular solution was often advocated as being the only one which merited the description of Christian. He was severely criticized for what he had said and was charged with giving his approval to all manner of social evils, such as apartheid and racism. Perhaps he did not make himself as clear as he should, though he believed that, as in the past, he had made very evident his abhorrence of apartheid as evil. The point he was trying to make was that, if the moral laws are made relative, the absolute authority is transferred to man-made solutions, about which, since they are necessarily imperfect, there can properly be a difference of judgement. Apartheid is an evil because it infringes a fundamental moral law, but it is legitimate for a Christian to maintain, for example, that sanctions *or* constructive and critical involvement is the best way

185

to combat it. It is illegitimate to try to enforce one or the other as the *only* Christian policy. Nor can any Christian maintain that those who adhere to the other view than that which he adopts are condoning the evil of apartheid and forfeit the right to be called Christians.

This experience serves to illustrate the way in which, in spite of our tradition of democracy, we have been affected by the approach of ideological politics. In many spheres, such as those of marriage, or abortion, the moral law has been abandoned and what is right, and therefore permissible, is identified with what the law permits. That is determined not by reference to a moral law but by an ideological view of what is thought to make people happiest in this life.

How, then, is the social gospel to be desecularized? In the situation which I have described, it is first necessary to emphasize that the Church and individual Christians must embrace wholeheartedly the obligation laid upon them by the gospel to be concerned with man's social and physical condition and his needs. The fact that the gospel is based upon the incarnation must exclude any form of dualism which restricts Christian concern to the spiritual sphere. Failure to embrace the material will inevitably mean that those who reject ideological politics will be accused of escapism and of neglecting the social ills of our time.

COMMITMENT TO UNIVERSAL MORAL LAW

The second requirement is that the Church should make its commitment to the universal moral law unequivocally clear and insist on the need for all political and social policies to be judged by it. This will not be easy in the Church of England, for in consideration of its own problems, the General Synod has been deeply infected by ideological politics. Not only does it claim something like infallibility in its treatment of doctrine. When it comes to an issue such as marriage, the emphasis is not on the teaching of our Lord but on the need to find a political way of accommodating its practice to those who have departed from it. The ideology is that of providing happiness in the world and the moral law, as the norm, is regarded as secondary to this. True compassion can only be exercised if the moral law is clearly made evident and accepted.

A simple example from the medical sphere serves to illustrate the point. A doctor when dealing with a patient has to deal with someone who, by the very fact of being a patient, has departed from what is known to be the normal condition of a human being. If the doctor is to be able to diagnose the condition and treat it properly, he must know what the normal condition is, against which the patient's condition is to be judged and to which he is committed to try to restore him. This acceptance of the norm on the part of the doctor must also be known to and recognized by the patient. If it is not, the patient will not trust the doctor and will be concerned to know by what criteria the doctor is acting. Will the doctor, for example, simply tell the patient that his condition need not worry him or that he must just accept it? The exercise of medical care demands for its proper operation that it is publicly accepted by all concerned that a doctor works from the normal, assesses the patients by it and works their restoration to it. At the same time, the doctor has to accept the condition in which he finds the patient and may have to accept that what he can do for him immediately is limited. He has to recognize that he cannot force the patient instantly back to normality. If the patient is seriously wounded, treatment for shock, stopping the bleeding, blood trans- fusions and drips may be all that is possible initially until the patient is in a suitable condition for further treatment. But if this be the situation, no one supposes that the doctor is acquiescing in the patient's condition or regarding it as normal.

In the sphere of the moral law, the public recognition of moral absolutes is necessary if compassion and care is to be properly exercised towards those in need and if they are to be provided without encouraging the idea that the condition of those in need is normal.

In the political sphere, it means that any policy or action must always be judged by the moral absolutes of natural law and must never be regarded as expressing it perfectly and therefore never to be questioned. It can only determine the legality of behaviour and can never determine whether it is morally right or wrong, but in legislation, politicians must take account of moral standards and legislation must always be directed to what is morally right and good, never just to what is expedient. It is the responsibility of the Church and of the Christian in politics, to assess any proposed policy or action by this criterion.

The third requirement for the descularization of the social gospel is the recognition of human freedom and of the need for any social action to be directed at whatever level to encouraging the exercise of that freedom in a responsible way. To act in a way which makes a human being the purely passive recipient of help and which denies mature responsibility is to violate one of the basic characteristics of a human being and to fail to respect human dignity. It is, in fact, to reduce a person to nothing more than an object for the satisfaction of the needs of others, however laudable their intentions may be.

THE NEED FOR GRACE AND THE HOPE OF HEAVEN

Above all, the Church and individual Christians must base their social concern on Christian doctrine and on the need for grace. It is often pointed out that St Paul, for example, always sees Christian behaviour as derivative from doctrine. Having expounded what God has done in Christ, he then says 'wherefore' or 'for the cause' Christians should behave in this or that way. At the same time, it is basic to St Paul's thoughts that to live as a Christian means living truly as a human being. In so doing, he reflects the moral teaching of our Lord, who addresses it to human beings, as such, created by God in his own image.

The Church must, therefore, simultaneously proclaim the gospel and its moral demands unequivocally and fearlessly, and make evident how to enable human nature in all its aspects to be fulfilled. In its proper involvement in the political sphere, it must, because of the insistence on the need for grace and the inability of man to save himself, judge what can rightly be expected of those who do not profess Christian belief and what can properly be required of society as a whole. This it must do without abandoning moral absolutes and without appearing to accept a relativist view of morals.

Finally, the Church and Christians need to give much greater and deeper content to the Christian hope of heaven. It is inevitable that when the Church's understanding of human destiny is thin and weak, there will be temptations to substitute some secular end. The influence of ideological politics lays this obligation upon the Church as a matter of extreme urgency. Failure to respond to it will inevitably mean that man and society will aim at a destiny which falls far short of what is proper to human nature or is contrary to it.

The remarkable passage in chapter 8 of St Paul's Letter to the Romans in which the reality of the world as it is, and the Christian hope, are blended in a creative way, provides the basis both for the exposition of that hope and the social concern of the Church.

I consider that the sufferings of this present time are not worth comparing with the glory that is to be revealed to us. For the creation waits with eager longing for the revealing of the sons of God; for the creation was subjected to futility, not of its own will but by the will of him who subjected it in hope; because the creation itself will be set free from its bondage to decay and obtain the glorious liberty of the children of God. We know that the whole creation has been groaning in travail together until now; and not only the creation, but we ourselves, who have the first fruits of the Spirit, groan inwardly as we wait for adoption as sons, the redemption of our bodies.[12]

NOTES

1   See p. 14.
2   BSR Publications.
3   Op. cit., para. 7.
4a *The Other Side of 1984* (Geneva 1984), p. 8.
4b G. Ionescu, *Politics and the Pursuit of Happiness*, (Harlow 1984), p. 8.
5   Ionescu, op. cit., p. 65.
6   T. S. Eliot, *The Rock* (London 1934), p. 42.
7   Ionescu, op. cit., p. 10.
8   Op. cit., p. 11.
9   Op. cit., pp. 11–12.
10 *The Dilemma of Democracy* (London 1978). pp. 10–13.
11 See 'Is Christianity Credible?' ed. David Stacey (London 1981), pp. 54–63.
12 Romans 8.18–23 (RSV).

INDEX OF NAMES

191

Index